How to Stop Your Child Smoking

Allen Carr

PENGUIN BOOKS

PENGUIN BOOKS

Published by the Penguin Group
Penguin Books Ltd, 27 Wrights Lane, London w8 5tz, England
Penguin Putnam Inc., 375 Hudson Street, New York, New York 10014, USA
Penguin Books Australia Ltd, Ringwood, Victoria, Australia
Penguin Books Canada Ltd, 10 Alcorn Avenue, Toronto, Ontario, Canada m4v 3b2
Penguin Books (NZ) Ltd, Private Bag 102902, NSMC, Auckland, New Zealand

Penguin Books Ltd, Registered Offices: Harmondsworth, Middlesex, England

First published 1999
10 9 8 7 6 5 4 3 2 1

Set in 11/14pt Monotype Bembo
Typeset by Rowland Phototypesetting Ltd, Bury St Edmunds, Suffolk
Printed in England by Clays Ltd, St Ives plc

CONTENTS

Smoking is so commonplace that we believe we know all there is to know about it. The truth is, that even in this so-called enlightened age, the really important facts are the complete opposite to what is generally accepted by the vast majority of Western society.

At one time 80 per cent of the adult population of the UK were smokers. The latest official statistics are 26 per cent. You could be excused for believing that we are gradually winning the war against the dreaded 'weed'. As far as adults are concerned I believe we are. However, there is one age group where smoking is actually on the increase and it's the group that you would least expect. I was about to say teenagers. Would that it were just teenagers. The truth is that there are literally thousands of 8- to 12-year-olds already hooked on nicotine. Why? After all, *we* didn't know about the cancer scares, no way would we have fallen for the trap had we known. So why do so many of our children get hooked? And why is smoking more prevalent among young girls?

Perhaps you are more concerned about your child becoming addicted to heavier drugs such as heroin. If so, you need to bear in mind that smoking is the thin end of the wedge. Before we start smoking we can enjoy social occasions and handle stress without any outside props. It is nicotine and to a lesser extent alcohol that train our bodies and minds to believe that we are incomplete. Because the beneficial effects of both drugs are illusory, it's little wonder that youngsters search for more powerful illusions.

The biggest misconception about the facts of smoking is society's attitude towards it. OK, so we know it's unhealthy and can lead to awful diseases, and even the majority of smokers now regard it as a filthy, unsociable pastime, but surely nothing like as bad as heroin addiction. Look at the facts: heroin kills less than 100 people annually in the UK. **SMOKING KILLS OVER 2,000 EVERY WEEK!**

Heroin is illegal. Smoking is not only legal, but we allow the tobacco industry to spend £100,000,000 per annum on tobacco advertising and promotion, and our own Treasury is the biggest vested interest, collecting around £10,000,000,000 per annum from the misery of smokers.

I'm not saying that most smokers end up taking harder drugs. What I am saying is, only a tiny percentage of drug addicts never smoked and if you prevent your child from smoking, he or she is unlikely to become a drug addict. This book will show you how to achieve that object. Do you merely give the book to your child? No, you read the book yourself.

1 Niagara Falls

I've always slept in the altogether. The first thing I used to do when I awoke every morning was to light a cigarette. I would be standing there stark naked, cigarette dangling from the side of my mouth, Humphrey Bogart style, 2 stones over-weight, grey complexion, pot-bellied, coughing and spluttering, fighting for breath. Not a pretty sight. No wonder I avoided the mirrors in our bedroom.

One of those holier-than-thou ex-smokers had a simple solution to my problem:

Why don't you try what I did? It didn't matter whether it was summer or winter, I'd jump out of bed every morning, and instead of lighting a cigarette, I'd throw open the window and take 10 deep breaths. Do that and there's no way you'll want to light a cigarette.

I thanked him for his advice and gave a half-hearted promise that I'd give it a try. There was no point in trying to explain to the idiot that the first deep breath would have sent me into paroxysms of coughing and that by the third deep breath, I would either have swallowed my cigarette or burned the carpet.

Non-smokers suffer the illusion that it is the heavy smokers who really enjoy smoking and casual smokers just do it for effect. As with practically every other aspect of smoking, the obvious is the opposite to the reality. Heavy smokers hate smoking and no longer suffer the illusion that they enjoy it. They might not admit this to other people, some cannot even admit it to themselves.

I cannot tell you the number of conversations I've had during which smokers wax lyrical about how much they enjoy the taste of tobacco. Ask them what taste has to do with it since they don't actually eat the tobacco and they'll tell you it has a wonderful smell. Point out that you can smell tobacco without actually breathing the cancerous fumes into your lungs and they will evade the issue by telling you how it relieves boredom and helps them to concentrate, how they like to smoke during both stressful situations and relaxing situations like after a meal or when socializing.

Point out to them that boredom and concentration are complete opposites, as are stressful and relaxing situations, and ask them to explain how the second cigarette out of the same packet can produce the exact opposite effect to the first and they will be unmoved. But ask them: 'Do your children smoke?' and if the answer is no, they won't be able to keep the smiles off their faces or hide how proud and relieved they feel because their children haven't become hooked. You say to them: 'Look, you've spent the last hour telling me of all the wonderful joys of being a smoker, why on earth would you want to deprive your children of those pleasures?' and the smoker is now non-plussed. In one sentence you have exploded all his previous arguments and he knows it. I've yet to meet a parent who likes the thought of his or her children smoking or a child that likes the thought of his or her parents smoking.

For years I had been chain-smoking 60 to 100 cigarettes a day. I would actually look forward to getting home from the office every evening just to give my lungs a rest. Provided I had no physical or mental work to do, I would lie on the settee watching television and was quite happy not to smoke. However, if I had to work late I had to continue chain-smoking. Occasionally, if I worked very late, I would run out of cigarettes. Just as if you ask directions of one of the locals in a strange town, if he's a drinking man, the landmarks will be 'The King's Head' and 'The George and Dragon', so if I ran out of cigarettes, I knew every all-night garage within a 5-mile radius.

On such nights I'd be hoping that I could complete my tasks, not so much because I was fed up with the work, but mainly so that I could stop punishing my lungs. I would lie in bed, tongue coated, throat feeling like a piece of emery paper, chest wheezing, either praying that the next morning I would wake up with sufficient willpower to quit, or desperately hoping that the desire to smoke would miraculously disappear.

I'd several times heard of smokers who, for no apparent reason, suddenly lost the urge to smoke. Why I was waiting for willpower I don't know, I knew I was strong-willed.

I am aware that youngsters and parents reading this book will find it difficult to relate to what I am saying. Even heavy smokers who are not far from the stage I had reached still console themselves with the thought: 'No wonder Allen Carr quit. If I had reached that stage, I would have quit.'

Falling into the smoking trap is like bathing on a hot summer's day in a cool, slow-moving river. Imperceptibly the speed of the current increases. The sensation is quite pleasant. There's no need to be perturbed. You are suddenly aware of a distant rumble. You realize that the current is quite fast. You swim for the bank, the speed of the current increases, you begin to panic, you are now hurtling along struggling to stay afloat. On the bank a sign flashes by:

DANGER NIAGARA FALLS!

You think I over-dramatize? Why do you think a smoker will have his leg removed rather than quit? Why do you think over 2,000 UK citizens die every week because they started smoking? How are 2,000 youngsters a week persuaded to take their place?

You need to understand the 'hows' and the 'whys'. However, first you need to know about:

VICE VERSA

Today's parents are shocked and distraught when they discover that their child smokes. It doesn't seem to make any difference whether the parents themselves are smokers or non-smokers. The non-smoking parents take the attitude: 'I just can't understand you, we've set you a good example, we've explained the horrendous diseases that can be caused by smoking. How could you be so stupid?'

The smoking parents are even more incredulous: 'I've told you what a stupid, filthy, disgusting, unhealthy waste of money it is. How could you be so stupid?' Of course, added to the incredulity is the guilt that smoking parents feel by not having set a good example. The do-gooders have added to this guilt complex by persuading smoking parents that their children only get hooked because of the example of their parents. If you are one of these guilt-ridden parents, I'm happy to tell you that the reasons why youngsters get hooked have practically nothing to do with whether their parents smoked or not.

When I first started stop-smoking clinics, I would ask the question: 'Do your parents smoke?' If they did the smoker would usually reply: 'Yes. So it was only natural for me to start.' If the parents were non-smokers, the reply would be something like: 'No. I believe I started just to rebel against my parents.'

It's weird how so many youngsters nowadays use the 'rebel' excuse to justify their smoking. In the bad old days the complete opposite would be our justification: 'Oh, I only smoke to be sociable.' What could be more unsociable than breathing disgusting fumes into the face of non-smokers while they are trying to enjoy a meal? You might just as well fart in their face and when they protest say: 'I was only trying to be sociable!'

Now that smoking is generally accepted as being anti-social, youngsters justify their apparent stupidity with: 'I'm a bit of a rebel. I like to oppose the normal trend.' It's a bit like 'Beatle mania', we would all wear 'Beatle'-type haircuts and suits and claim that we liked to be different from the crowd. Usually when a youngster tells you he smokes because he's a rebel, he's surrounded by a dozen other rebels all puffing away. I have the greatest respect for rebels. But what are they actually rebelling against? I admire someone who rebels against slavery, or against other evils, but how can you be a rebel *for* slavery, particularly your own slavery? These rebellious youngsters are in exactly the same situation as that puppet of the tobacco industry, 'FOREST':

Freedom Organization for the Right to Enjoy Smoking Tobacco

It's the only organization I know that fights for a freedom that it already has and always has had. Forest is an excellent name for it. If ever there was an organization that was designed to prevent you from seeing the weed (sorry, slip of the tongue), the wood from the trees, this is it.

I would suggest that what youngsters really need is not 'FOREST' but 'FENS':

Freedom to Escape from Nicotine Slavery

If parents advised their children not to jump under a bus or off the edge of a cliff, how many youngsters would actually do it just to prove how rebellious they were, and even if the occasional odd-ball did and somehow survived the experience, would their friends treat them with respect or regard them as imbeciles? Do you not also find it an incredible coincidence that once these smoking youngsters realize that they have fallen into a trap and decide to escape from nicotine slavery, amazingly their rebellious natures seem to desert them and after a few days or weeks they find some feeble excuse to continue the slavery?

Did you ever read the book or see the film *Vice Versa*? It was about a young boy at boarding school who was transposed into his father's body and vice versa. It gave a great insight into the different perspectives of children and adults. In order to prevent your child from becoming hooked on drugs, you must do exactly the same. Of course you must use the knowledge and experience you have gained, but you must also be able to see it as your child would in order for your child to learn from your experience.

Let's consider a couple of typical examples where the child and the parent were on completely different wave-lengths. The first is of a 60-year-old father who had already had multiple by-pass operations and attended our London clinic with his 20-year-old son. It was obvious at the outset that the youngster had been dragged along by his father and had not the slightest intention of stopping smoking.

One of my greatest disappointments in life is that I have never learned the knack of whistling as youngsters do in American films. To be able to put two fingers in your mouth and let out an ear-piercing shriek must give tremendous satisfaction. When I've cured the world of smoking I'll try again. Now, you'd think that a man who had chain-smoked for nearly a third of a century would have discovered the art of blowing perfect smoke rings. I never did. Whilst the remainder of the group, including the father, were absorbed in what I was saying, I was absorbed with his son who sat blowing the most perfect smoke rings one after the other. I have to admit that I was quite impressed with the quality of those smoke rings.

Unfortunately the father spotted his son, who was engrossed with his skill and clearly not listening to a word I was saying. It was somewhat embarrassing. In front of the assembled company he began to harangue his son. I confess that I do not remember his exact words but it was to the effect: 'How dare you sit there blowing smoke rings? You can see what smoking has done to me. Why don't you stop while you can?'

Fortunately the youngster didn't retaliate. But his expression spoke for itself: 'You silly old fool! You lecture me? I should be lecturing you! Fancy letting it get to that stage. That could never happen to me!'

The second case was of a man who telephoned me late at night. He was very distraught, in fact he was crying. He said: 'My doctor has told me that unless I stop smoking, I'll lose my legs. I'll pay you anything if you can stop me for a week. I know that if I can survive a week I'll be OK.'

The man was convinced that I wouldn't be able to help him but nevertheless he attended a group session and found it easy to stop. He sent me a nice thank-you letter and recommended me to several other smokers. Practically the last thing I say to ex-smokers leaving my clinic is: 'Remember, you must never smoke another cigarette!' This particular man said: 'Have no fear, Allen, if I manage to stop, I will never smoke again.'

It was obvious to me that my warning hadn't registered. I said: 'I know you think that at the moment, but in 6 months you will have forgotten.'

'Allen, I'll never smoke again.'

About a year later there was another phone call: 'Allen, I had just one small cigar at Christmas, I'm now back on 40 cigarettes a day.'

'Do you remember when you first phoned? You were so miserable, you were going to pay me anything if you could stop for a week.'

'I remember, haven't I been stupid?'

'Do you remember that letter you sent me? How

much fitter you felt and how nice it was to be free?'

'I know, I know.'

'Do you remember you promised me you'd never smoke again?'

'I know, I'm a fool.'

It's like finding someone up to their neck in a bog and about to go under. You help pull them out, they are so grateful to you, then 6 months later they dive straight back into the bog.

Ironically, when this man attended a subsequent session he said: 'Can you believe it? I offered to pay my son £1,000 if he hadn't smoked by his 21st birthday. I duly paid up, he's now 22 and puffing away like a chimney. Can you believe he could be so stupid when he's seen what smoking has done to me?'

I said: 'You think he's stupid? At least he avoided the trap for 21 years, and he didn't know the misery he was in for. You were in the trap for over 40 years. You had personal experience of the misery of being a smoker, yet you only managed to stay free for a year!'

It is essential that I digress for a moment. There are bound to be smokers, ex-smokers or even non-smokers (people who have never fallen for the trap), whether they be young or old, who will be thinking: 'No, he might not have smoked for a year, but no way was he free – once a smoker, always a smoker, you might never smoke again, but you'll never be completely free!'

I have much sympathy with this belief. Before I discovered my method I was convinced of its truth and that the vast majority of smokers that quit with a method that involves the use of willpower never feel completely free. The belief is reinforced by the millions of smokers who haven't smoked for years but still crave the occasional cigarette, and by the millions of smokers who quit for months or even years and get hooked again. **ALL** smokers, including youngsters, wish they had never started, even though most of them are not prepared to admit it.

The usual excuse we give for continuing to smoke is that we enjoy it so much. Incredibly we never do. The reason we believe we enjoy it is that we get in a panic and feel miserable whenever we are not allowed to smoke and it is only to avoid this feeling of deprivation and misery that any smoker takes the next shot of nicotine.

There are two major factors that make us continue to smoke and neither is that we enjoy it. The first is that we believe we have to go through some terrible trauma of indeterminate length in order to quit. The irony is that the vast majority of smokers actually go through that trauma on one or more occasions during their smoking lives and do actually succeed in becoming reasonably happy non-smokers for a period of weeks, months or even years. But they don't feel completely free and sooner or later the vast majority get hooked again. This is the major reason why an attempt to quit will strike terror into the hearts of the bravest of smokers: a belief that even if you survive the misery of the transitional period of indeterminate length, you still won't be completely free – you'll never completely enjoy a meal again or be able to cope with stress again without a cigarette.

It is necessary to explode this myth before getting back to the examples of *Vice Versa*. You might well argue that the second example confirms the myth: if the father was really free, why did he get hooked again after a year?

I promise you that he was free. Unfortunately, no matter which system a smoker uses to quit smoking, including mine which makes the process easy, even enjoyable, all too many get hooked again. I said to this man as I've said to many others: 'Did you find it easy to quit?'

'I didn't even have any withdrawal pangs, I was on cloud nine!'

'Did you enjoy being a non-smoker?'

'It was like being released from prison, like waking up from a nightmare, escaping from a drugged black and white world of fear and depression into a world of health, sunshine and freedom.'

'Do you enjoy being a smoker again?'

'I loathe it! Why do you think I've come back to see you?'

So why did he get hooked again? Remember, this is a digression, all I'm trying to establish is the fact that he *was* actually free. The reason he got hooked again is because nicotine addiction is not only prevalent, but is the most ingenious, subtle, sinister trap that man and nature have combined to lay. He got caught again for exactly the same reason that he got caught in the first place, and that his son got caught and that your child got caught or is likely to get caught unless between us you, I and society generally do something to eliminate nicotine addiction. Ironically, it is not an infectious disease in the true sense of the word, but is in effect more contagious than any disease in the whole history of the human race.

However, that is a subject we will deal with later. The object of this chapter is to help overcome the generation gap. Let me remind you of the two examples I gave: the first of the son blowing smoke rings in the presence of a father who had ruined his health through smoking; the second, a son who had remained free for 21 years and a father who had abstained for a year, but all four firmly entrapped.

The above are examples of situations where both parent and child are speaking the same language, but they aren't communicating.

The generation gap isn't easy to overcome, but with the use of imagination, sensitivity and psychology it can be done. One of the difficulties of being a parent is that we feel protective towards our children. It's only natural that we don't want them to make the same mistakes that we did. The problem is that in order to protect them it is sometimes necessary to discipline them. Conversations can all too easily become lectures or even reprimands and when that happens communication is non-existent.

If you are a smoker or an ex-smoker, it is far better to explain how you got lured into the trap, rather than lecture your children on the evils of smoking. If you've never been a smoker, arrange a conversation between your child and a smoker or ex-smoker whom you know they respect – someone who will also not lecture them but explain in honest and simple terms how they were lured into the trap and how they wished they had never lit that first cigarette.

If you can first understand the position of your children and are speaking the same language on equal terms, then communication will be taking place. However, there is no point in establishing communication if you are communicating the wrong messages. To establish communication is one essential. Another is to:

AVOID COMPLACENCY

3 *Avoid Complacency*

It is very easy to under-estimate the subtlety of the nicotine trap. Nowadays children are taught in school to lecture their smoking parents about the evils of smoking. It's another form of *Vice Versa*. When I was a boy our parents used to lecture us.

I remember one amusing story of a young housewife who attended our clinic. Every night her 5-year-old daughter would conclude her prayers: 'Please help Mummy to stop smoking so she doesn't die.' Understandably, the young lady had made a valiant attempt to quit, but it was doomed to failure. She had reached the stage whereby she wouldn't smoke during the day, but would have one or two cigarettes in the evening after her daughter was safely asleep.

On one occasion, the housewife had had a particularly bad day and was really looking forward to that cigarette. But in strict accordance with Sod's Law, her daughter, who normally invariably dropped off within 5 minutes of her head hitting the pillow, took over an hour. The lady said: 'The moment her eyes closed I rushed down to the kitchen and lit up. No sooner had I lit up than there was a small voice behind me saying, "You aren't smoking, are you, Mummy?"' Can you imagine how that lady felt, caught out by her 5-year-old daughter, stealing the jam red-handed?

The important point that I am making is that all youngsters hate smoking before they become hooked. There isn't a child on the planet that likes the thought of their parents smoking and there isn't a parent on the planet that likes the thought of their children smoking.

That's not surprising when you look at the cold hard facts about smoking. Let's do that. The only reason that anyone starts in the first place is all the other people doing it. Yet every one of those smokers wishes that they had never started. They even warn us not to be stupid. Eventually we try one. It tastes awful. All our lives smokers have been telling us that they smoke because they enjoy a cigarette. So we are fooled into thinking that while we don't enjoy them, we won't get hooked. We work so hard to get hooked, then spend the rest of our lives with our heads buried in the sand trying to block our minds to the fact that we are smoking, or at odd times attempting to get free and telling our own children not to be stupid. The average 20-a-day smoker now spends over £40,000 on smoking in a lifetime. An absolute fortune! Yet even smokers who can't afford to smoke say: 'I'm not worried about the money.' Why aren't we worried about the money? Why do we shop around to save a pound on essentials, yet block our minds to the money we waste on cigarettes?

But it's what we do with that money that is so frightening. We actually use it to risk horrendous diseases. OK, we console ourselves with the thought that it won't happen to us, or we'll stop long before it gets to that stage. Even if we do get away with it, we sentence ourselves to a lifetime of bad breath, stained teeth, misery and lethargy. Why does the sheer slavery never dawn on us? We smoke most of our cigarettes without even being aware that we are smoking. In fact the only times we are aware of it are those times when we are coughing and spluttering and wishing that we had never started, or when we are breathing smoke into the face of a non-smoker and feeling stupid and unclean. The only other times that we are aware that we are smokers is when we are getting low on cigarettes and that panic feeling starts, or we are in situations where society will not allow us to smoke and we are feeling deprived and miserable.

WHAT SORT OF HOBBY OR PLEASURE IS IT THAT WHEN YOU ARE ALLOWED TO DO IT, YOU ARE EITHER NOT AWARE THAT YOU ARE DOING IT OR IF YOU ARE AWARE, WISH THAT YOU DIDN'T AND IT'S ONLY WHEN YOU ARE NOT ALLOWED TO DO IT THAT IT SEEMS SO PRECIOUS?

It's a lifetime of being pitied and despised by other people. But the very worst aspect of being a smoker is that it's a lifetime of otherwise intelligent, happy, healthy, attractive human beings having to go through life despising themselves, every Budget Day, every cancer scare, every time their family give them that haunted look, every time they are not allowed to smoke, or are the lone smoker in the presence of non-smokers.

It's well worth memorizing the last 4 paragraphs and the next 2 parrot-fashion and the next time a smoker, young or old, casual or heavy, tells you they smoke because they choose to, just reel those paragraphs off to them.

Of course they'll try to justify the down-side by reciting the compensations on the other side of the tug-of-war: how smoking relieves stress and boredom, and assists concentration and relaxation. However, not only does smoking not do any of these things, it is a major cause of stress and boredom and actually impedes relaxation and concentration.

If you are a smoker, you might question the truth of the last paragraph. I will explain later how the illusion occurs. But what you cannot dispute is that before you became hooked on nicotine, you had neither need nor desire to smoke a cigarette in order to relax or concentrate or to relieve stressful or boring situations. It is absolutely ludicrous to suggest that anyone would actually choose to become a smoker or that such a lifestyle could be described as pleasurable. The biggest imbecile on the planet wouldn't choose to become a smoker, let alone a rational intelligent human being, which the vast majority of smokers are.

But it is just because our children hated the smell of tobacco, because they know the horrendous diseases that smoking leads to, because they lectured us about those evils, because the disadvantages of being a smoker are so obvious and predominant:

WE BECOME COMPLACENT!

It is this very complacency that is the greatest ally of the nicotine trap. Stop kidding yourself. Take your head out of the sand:

LOOK AT THE FACTS!

It is a fact that over 100,000 youngsters are becoming hooked every year in the UK alone. What makes you think that your child is immune? Because they've lectured you about the evils? Because they hate the smell? Because you've explained the dangers of smoking to them? Stop kidding yourself, the same facts apply to every one of them, but still over 2,000 get hooked every week.

Perhaps you are complacent because your child hasn't become hooked? If so, you are the equivalent of the man who, having fallen from the 100-storey sky-scraper, is heard to say as he hurtles past the 10th storey: 'So far so good.'

There are literally thousands of youngsters and smokers in their 20s whose parents haven't the slightest idea that their children are hooked. There is nothing more devious, inventive and ingenious than the mind of an addict.

The official statistics of teenage smoking are frightening, particularly with young girls: 1 in 3 are smoking by the age of 15. Perhaps this doesn't particularly perturb you as you are so confident in the case of your own child that she will be one of the abstainers.

One in 3 at the age of 15 is shocking enough. But I

have learned to question statistics about smokers, no matter how honest and meticulous the intention of the compilers.

It is important to remember that all drug addicts lie about their addiction. It is also important to remember that, whereas it is possible to prove that an individual smokes, it is impossible to prove that a particular individual doesn't smoke. Throughout my years of fighting the tobacco industry, at odd times I've been told of rumours that Allen Carr is smoking again. I've never been able to track down the source of these rumours, but I cannot describe the frustration of not being able to do so.

Some years ago I was asked to speak to a group of teenagers at a famous girls' school in the expectation that I could coax those who had already become hooked into quitting and help those who had yet to become hooked from falling into the trap.

I was already sceptical about the 1 in 3 official statistics. My home at Raynes Park lay directly between a large residential population and the local girls' school. It seemed to me that every one of those girls was puffing away on the way to school and on the way back.

At the girls' school I wanted the girls to feel that they could talk freely. I therefore insisted that there were no teachers present. It was a brave request on my part. I was already aware of the generation gap and that these girls would regard me as just another old fogey who had been sent to bore them about the evils of smoking. My only previous knowledge of girls' schools was obtained from films about St Trinian's. I'm not a particularly brave person and I confess that the bravest act of my life was to stand before 150 to 160 12- to 15-year-olds.

I have the greatest respect for those girls. It wouldn't have taken much effort on their part to have destroyed me. I was already under the impression that it was practically impossible to help teenagers to see the light. But it was the incredibly honest and mature attitude of those girls that has given me the resolve to write this book and the hope that we can prevent our children from falling for the evil trap of drug addiction. Because, unless we can prevent youngsters from falling into the trap, we will never eliminate that trap.

Instead of asking how many of those girls were smokers, I did it the other way around. I said: 'I've heard that there are people who have never ever smoked a cigarette in their lives. Now, I find this difficult to believe. Surely everyone has tried one cigarette in their life even if it was just out of curiosity. If any of you have never ever smoked a single cigarette would you please raise your hand.'

About 10 girls raised their hands. This was about what I had expected. I then asked them to lower their hands and for the remainder to raise theirs.

My next question was: 'If you had just the one cigarette and never smoked another, would you please lower your hand.' I was fully expecting half the hands to be lowered immediately. What actually happened was that of the 150 girls who had their hands raised, only about 10 lowered their hands and in most cases after a pause.

I confess to being somewhat shocked. I admit that I had been sceptical of the official statistics of 1 in 3, but even I found it difficult to accept what I was seeing.

I asked the girls to put their arms down. My next question was: 'If you believe that you are hooked on nicotine, please raise your arm.' I had made a mistake. I should have asked the opposite: 'If you smoke and don't believe that you are hooked on nicotine, raise your arm.' I'm not able to tell what the result would have been. But in answer to the question that I actually asked, I wouldn't have expected one girl to raise her arm.

In fact about 10 girls raised their arms including one 12-year-old. Their honesty was greeted by giggles from the remainder of the audience. I said: 'You are laughing at them, in reality they should be laughing at you, at least they have had the intelligence to realize that they are hooked.' The truth is that the 10 were in fact less hooked than the remainder. Once you realize that you are in a trap at least you have a desire to escape and therefore have some chance of escape. If you don't realize that you have been trapped, you have no desire to escape and no chance of success.

The purpose of this chapter is to remove any complacency you might have about your child becoming hooked. Even the 10 girls who had resisted the temptation of that first experimental cigarette weren't safe, nor were the handful of girls who tried just one. That was no guarantee that some of them won't get hooked at a later date. The danger doesn't end with adolescence, it's there throughout life. A new boyfriend, a different set of friends, a new job, there's a multitude of factors that can trick a youngster or adult into trying just one cigarette.

At the clinics we regularly have clients who didn't get hooked until their 30s, 40s or 50s. There is no age at which a youngster or adult can be considered safe from falling into the nicotine trap. Unless of course you understand the trap completely. The main object of this work is to enable you to do just this and to ensure that your child also understands it. Let us now consider:

THE INCREDIBLE INGENUITY OF THE NICOTINE TRAP

4 *The Incredible Ingenuity of the Nicotine Trap*

First understand the purpose of any trap. It is simply that – to trap you. A secondary purpose of the nicotine trap is to keep you trapped for life. One of the ingenious subtleties of the trap is to make you believe that you are in control: that you are smoking because you choose to and that you choose to because you get some form of genuine pleasure or crutch from smoking.

You are aware of the risks. Peer pressure and tobacco advertising might try to persuade you to smoke, but nobody can force you to do it. After all, you are a man or woman of the world, you don't actually believe that the improved version of your favourite washing powder washes whiter than white. They've been making that claim for over 20 years. How can anything wash whiter than white?

So the first essential to understanding the nature of the nicotine trap is to realize that no smokers choose to smoke. It is true that we choose to try our first experimental cigarettes, but as I have explained in the previous chapter, the biggest idiot on earth wouldn't choose to become hooked on nicotine. You chose to read this book. But you didn't choose to spend the rest of your life reading it.

Fortunately most smokers can remember how foul

those first cigarettes tasted and how hard they had to work in order to learn to inhale. The reason the cigarettes tasted foul is that tobacco contains many poisonous compounds.

Every human being instinctively knows from the foul smell and taste of that first cigarette that there is something evil and unnatural about breathing those lethal fumes into our lungs. So why do we smoke the second cigarette? Because of peer pressure? This is often given as the excuse, but if my friends were sticking needles into their veins loaded with heroin, I don't think that would make me want to do it.

Do we want to smoke the second cigarette because we know it's an acquired taste and that if we persevere we'll learn to enjoy smoking? This doesn't make sense either. It would mean that we actually planned at the outset to become hooked. Nobody decides to become hooked or dependent on a drug, whether it be nicotine, alcohol, heroin or whatever.

In a sense smokers are already hooked by the first cigarette. Of course they don't realize it at the time, any more than the fish that takes the angler's bait, or the fly that is lured into a pitcher-plant and begins to imbibe the nectar. Whether it be smoker, fish or fly, it is not until the victim tries to escape that it realizes that it is trapped. In the case of the fish it doesn't take long. With the fly it takes somewhat longer. In the case of the smoker, it usually takes years, in fact many smokers have lived and died in the mistaken belief that they only smoke because they choose to.

Probably the most ingenious aspect of the nicotine trap is that cigarettes taste and smell foul. If the trap were identical to the pitcher-plant, if those first cigarettes tasted marvellous, alarm bells would ring. We are intelligent human beings, we would see immediately why 80 per cent of the adult population were at one time hooked on tobacco and we would heed the warning. But not only does that first cigarette not taste like nectar, it actually tastes foul.

Our defences are down. Any latent fear that we might have had about becoming hooked has been removed. No way could we ever become hooked on these filthy things.

Youngsters believe they don't become hooked until they learn to enjoy the taste and smell of tobacco. The tiny minority that either through fear, intelligence or instinct never try that first experimental cigarette, refuse to take the bait. The vast majority that, for whatever reason, sooner or later, try that experimental cigarette, have taken the bait. Whether they become hooked or not has little to do with intelligence. Some youngsters find that first cigarette so repulsive that they are not prepared to go through the considerable learning process required to inhale without having a coughing fit or feeling sick, to feel like the tough guy or the sophisticated adult or to *acquire* the taste.

In fact you never acquire the taste. Whether it be cigarette, pipe or cigar, no matter what the brand of the tobacco, all that smokers do is train their brains and bodies to become immune to the poisons of the particular brand of tobacco that they are smoking. It's rather like working on a pig farm: after a while you become immune to the smell of the pigs.

However, if the youngster tries the second cigarette, he or she is already hooked. The ingenious trap has claimed another victim.

Let's take a closer look at:

THE MECHANICS OF THE NICOTINE TRAP

5 *The Mechanics of the Nicotine Trap*

Before we start smoking we don't *need* cigarettes. We are quite capable of coping with stress and can enjoy social occasions. With a drug like cocaine one sniff is one shot of the drug. But when you smoke nicotine each puff is one shot of the drug. When you take that first puff you put nicotine into the body. I must dispel the mistaken belief that you won't get hooked if you don't inhale. For most of our lives we are not conscious that we are breathing air into our lungs, but obviously we do. That first puff will taste awful. Immediately the nicotine will start to leave your body. This creates an empty, insecure feeling which is identical to normal stress and normal hunger. The second puff will also taste awful. However, it will also replace the nicotine and that empty, insecure feeling will also be replaced by a feeling of confidence, relaxation, security, satisfaction or whatever you like to call it.

Of course both the insecure feeling and its relief are so imperceptible at the time that the youngster won't even be aware of it. But youngsters do actually feel less nervous or more confident when they take that second puff. They aren't consciously aware of it but their brains are, and are fooled into believing that it was a genuine boost. In fact the boost was merely partially removing the feeling of insecurity that the first puff had created.

There are many pathetic aspects to smoking, but the most pathetic of all is that the actual pleasure or crutch a smoker receives when they light up is to get back to the level of confidence and relaxation they felt before they lit that first cigarette, in other words to feel like a non-smoker.

Smokers believe that they suffer physical withdrawal pangs from nicotine when they attempt to quit smoking. In fact smokers suffer them throughout their smoking lives and it's the only reason that any smoker, young or old, casual or heavy, lights the next cigarette.

Now, whether you are a smoker, a non-smoker or an ex-smoker, you might find the above explanation rather simplistic and difficult to believe. Surely if it were that simple smokers would realize that the crutch or pleasure they get is just an illusion, equivalent to wearing tight shoes in order to get the pleasure of removing them.

I assure you that it *is* just as simple as I have explained. The problem is that those simple facts have been confused and distorted to make the nicotine trap appear incredibly complicated. My claim to fame is that I was the first person to understand the true nature of the smoking trap. I hasten to add that the discovery was not through any genius on my part but merely as a result of the peculiar circumstances of my life.

If it is really as simple as I claim, why isn't it obvious to other smokers? There are several reasons for that. Let's examine them:

1. From birth our young brains are literally bombarded daily with information telling us that smoking does help to relieve boredom and stress, does assist concentration and relaxation. So when we take that second puff and experience that feeling ourselves, why should we even question it?

2. When we light our first cigarette we are already feeling nervous. The mere fact that it is our first cigarette will make us feel nervous. Childhood and adolescence are also comparatively nervous times in our lives. In any event the additional level of nervousness created by the nicotine leaving our bodies is so imperceptible that it is impossible to distinguish it from other causes. In fact, so slight is it, that throughout our smoking lives we only know the feeling as needing something to do with our hands or merely as 'I want a cigarette.'

3. It works back to front. It's when you are not smoking that you suffer the empty feeling. So you don't blame it on the previous cigarette. When you light up the empty feeling is immediately replaced with a feeling of relaxation. It is an ingenious, subtle trap. You can fool all of the people some of the time and some of the people all of the time. But you can't fool all of the people all of the time. I regret to say that is exactly what the nicotine trap has done for generations. Fortunately its days are now numbered.

Perhaps you still find the concept difficult to absorb? Can you picture how heroin addicts sink to the level of sticking needles into their veins? I was given the impression that it was because of the marvellous highs they obtained. There are other marvellous highs in life. Can you remember the excitement of Christmas or your birthday when you were a child? Have you experienced the pleasure of reliving that excitement through your children or grandchildren? Was that excitement preceded by a period of black depression? On the contrary, the preparation and anticipation of a high can often exceed the reality. Was the experience followed by a year's depression waiting for the next Christmas or birthday? Of course not; genuine highs are a pleasure in themselves and there is no corresponding depression.

Is that true of drug addiction? Now picture the misery of a heroin addict who has no heroin and the relief he obtains when at last he can plunge that needle into a vein. Do you really believe that is a high? Picture the shaking of an alcoholic when deprived of alcohol and the vomiting and pathetic misery, depression, aggression and degradation that follow when he obtains alcohol.

Do non-heroin addicts get into a panic when they have no heroin? Of course not, the thought of having to stick needles into their veins and of being dependent on that awful drug is sheer anathema to them. Heroin doesn't create highs, it merely creates lows. Do non-smokers get into a panic because they are not allowed to smoke? Of course not. They cannot understand how anyone could spend a fortune to risk horrendous diseases by sticking those filthy things in their mouths. And neither could any nicotine addict before falling into the trap.

Smokers believe that there is some genuine crutch or pleasure in smoking, purely for smoking's sake, and that the health scares, the lethargy, the money, the wheezing and coughing, the filth and the slavery are just annoying hazards that the smoker has to endure in order to enjoy the pleasure or to obtain the crutch.

Just think about it. Would you get pleasure from sticking a burning cigarette in your ear? Of course not. So why should smokers get pleasure from sticking the filthy things in their mouths? Because they enjoy the taste? Where does taste come into it? We don't eat cigarettes. Say to a smoker: 'If you can't get your own brand and can only obtain a brand you find distasteful, do you stop smoking?' No way, smokers will smoke old rope rather than nothing.

They might try to convince you that it's the wonderful smell which causes them to smoke. I think that most of us would agree that the perfume of a rose is far more pleasant than that of tobacco, but have you ever seen anyone trying to smoke rose-leaves? You don't have to smoke tobacco in order to smell it.

Some will tell you they smoke merely to have something to do with their hands. Suggest to them that it would be far less risky and much cheaper to fiddle with a biro and they'll look at you as if it's you that's stupid.

Others will tell you that they smoke to relieve boredom. Ask them what is so particularly mind-absorbing about sticking a cigarette in your mouth and setting light to it and they'll be hard put to find an answer.

Others will tell you that smoking helps them to concentrate. Ask them how it manages to do that and they'll be lost for an explanation. Some will tell you that their favourite cigarettes are when they are relaxing and that they find a cigarette also seems to help during stressful situations. Point out to them that relaxing situations and stressful situations are complete opposites, and so incidentally are boredom and concentration, and ask them to explain to you how an identical cigarette out of the same packet can have the completely opposite effect to the one they smoked an hour previously and they'll be at a loss.

Some otherwise intelligent human beings might also try to convince you that an identical cigarette out of the same packet will taste better at certain times, usually after a meal. However, if you tried to convince them that bacon and eggs tasted better after a cigarette, they would regard you as a fool.

Any long-term heavy smoker with an ounce of intelligence will already have discerned that the reasons smokers give to justify their smoking are not reasons but mere excuses. Eventually most of us reach the stage where we think we smoke because we've got into the habit and habits are difficult to break.

There are several misconceptions here. The first is that habits are difficult to break. Habits are easy to break providing that you are certain in your mind that you want to break them.

A classic example is that in the UK we habitually drive on the left-hand side of the road. However, if we visit the Continent or the States, we immediately switch to the right with little or no hassle and find it just as easy to return to the left when we arrive back in the UK.

The second misconception is that smoking is a habit. Unfortunately, many so-called specialists in drug addiction confuse the issue by using terms that are not synonymous. They'll refer to a heroin 'user', a heroin 'habit' or a heroin 'addict'. 'User' implies that the person is in control and can take it or leave it. 'Addict' implies that the victim has now completely lost control. 'Habit' implies an in-between stage: is he still a user or is he already an addict?

Get it clearly into your mind that drug addiction is not a habit but a cunning trap. Let's go back to the analogy of the fly lured into a pitcher-plant used in the previous chapter. It doesn't fly to the plant out of habit, but because it finds the smell of the nectar irresistible. It doesn't start eating the nectar out of habit but because the nectar tastes irresistible. At this stage the fly would regard itself as a 'user', it believes that it is in control, enjoying the nectar in the safe knowledge that it can fly away whenever it wants to. Isn't a young smoker who has learned to inhale tobacco smoke without coughing, who now believes that he smokes purely because he obtains some pleasure or crutch from smoking, in exactly the same position?

Eventually it will dawn on both the fly and the smoker that they are trapped. But when did they actually become trapped? In the case of the fly, it was the moment it first got the whiff of the nectar. In the case of the smoker, it was the moment he or she decided to smoke that first cigarette. I've no doubt that a minority of the small number of people who never light the experimental cigarette avoid doing so because, even though they don't understand the exact nature of the nicotine trap, they have the common sense to learn from the mistakes of their elders. However, I believe that the majority of them avoid it not because they are more intelligent or knowledgeable but out of fear.

This was all that prevented me from dabbling with harder drugs. It wasn't because I understood the nature of the trap, but because I had so rapidly capitulated to being completely dependent on nicotine that I was convinced that if I had experimented with anything harder I would have been dead within a few months.

Some youngsters are lucky enough never to smoke the next cigarette. Again you might argue: 'It wasn't just luck, they were more intelligent.' I can't agree. If they were more intelligent they wouldn't have needed to light the first one. The truth is that many youngsters find that first cigarette so repulsive that they immediately lose any desire to light another. It's really: 'There but for the grace of God go I.'

Let us assume for a moment that smoking is just a habit. Why should it be difficult to break? After all, no one can force us to smoke other than ourselves. If we decide on day one that we don't ever wish to smoke again, why should we find difficulty? After all, we don't even have to do anything, all we need to do is not light another cigarette.

But what about the awful physical pain caused by nicotine withdrawal? What awful physical pain? Question smokers who are attempting to quit when using the willpower method and ask them what actual terrible pains they are suffering, and they will waffle. The conversation usually goes something like this:

Q: You complain that you are suffering considerable pain. Can you be more specific? Where is it actually hurting you?

A: Oh, it's terrible, like flu.

Q: And your doctor has told you that is nicotine withdrawal?

A: Well no, I haven't actually been to my doctor.

Q: Don't you think you ought to? After all, if the symptoms are like flu, isn't it likely that you have flu?

A: No, I know it's because I've stopped smoking.

Q: Can you describe the symptoms?

A: I keep breaking out into cold sweats.

Q: Linford Christie does that every time he runs, but it doesn't seem to bother him. Why does it bother you?

A: But I'm finding it difficult to sleep at night.

Q: I often have periods when I find it difficult to sleep at night. I should imagine everyone does at various times in their lives. Is that really so horrendous?

You could also point out that if you said to a smoker: 'You can have flu for 5 days and afterwards you'll never have the slightest desire to smoke again,' the majority of smokers would jump at the opportunity. After all, when we have flu, physically we might feel as if we are dying, but we don't get all weepy and irritable, we just take it in our stride. The reason that smokers get so depressed when they attempt to quit has nothing to do with the physical withdrawal pain of nicotine. As I have already explained, it is so slight, almost imperceptible, we only know it as the feeling of 'I want a cigarette', and it disappears completely after a few days.

The torture that smokers suffer when they quit is fear and depression. They believe that they are making a genuine sacrifice. They believe that smoking is a genuine pleasure or crutch, that it genuinely helps to relieve boredom and stress and genuinely assists concentration and relaxation. If smokers believe that when they extinguish what they hope will be their final cigarette, they will spend the rest of their lives believing it. Every time in the future that they are bored, or cannot concentrate, or suffer stress, or when their smoking friends light up at social occasions, part of their brain will be saying: 'You are being deprived.' Sooner or later, probably sooner, they'll light just one cigarette and the nicotine chain will start again.

There is but one object to this chapter: to help you to understand that the only reason any smoker continues to light cigarettes is exactly the same reason that heroin addicts inject themselves with heroin – not because they get some genuine pleasure or high, but to try to end the empty, insecure feeling that the first dose of the drug started and the last dose perpetuated. It is exactly the same with nicotine.

Whether you are a smoker, ex-smoker or non-smoker, it is difficult to accept the concept that the only reason any smoker continues to smoke is to try to end the empty, insecure feeling that the previous cigarette perpetuated.

Imagine for a moment that you had been reading this book 200 years ago. I would have been saying: 'Look, there really is no pleasure in sniffing dust up your nose, the snuff is just tobacco, which contains nicotine, it's just your way of obtaining nicotine, but it's the nicotine that is causing your problem.'

There are already thousands of ex-smokers hooked on nicotine chewing gum, and many of them are still smoking cigarettes. Ex-smokers attend our clinics just to get off the chewing gum. In recent years there has been immense publicity about nicotine patches. We've already had a lady at the Raynes Park clinic who said: 'I take my patch off about three times a day so that I can have a cigarette with my husband and stick it back on with sticky tape.' Are we really going to have to ask clients in a few years' time: 'Now, be honest, how many patches a day are you on?' Will nicotine addicts in 20 years' time be bragging:

'I'm down to two patches a day!' or,

'I only wear them when I'm socializing,' or

'I don't need them, I enjoy them, what could be more relaxing than wearing a nice patch after a meal?'

If you think such comments are stretching the imagination, try to imagine the same comments about sniffing dust up your nose. That's the sort of comment that snuff-takers actually made to justify their stupidity. So why not patch-wearers?

Do you think that cocaine-sniffers do so because they enjoy sniffing? Of course not! That's how they take the drug. Snuff-takers sniffed for exactly the same reason – they were addicted to nicotine. Snuff-taking was once regarded as a sociable pastime. The truth was that, just like smoking, it was a filthy, disgusting addiction, but just as smokers would deceive themselves with gold and silver cigarette cases and lighters, so snuff-takers would attempt the same deception by using silver snuff-boxes.

Do you really believe that heroin addicts inject themselves because they enjoy injections? The only reason they do it is because they believe the heroin will relieve the empty, insecure feeling that the previous injection perpetuated. What they don't realize is that the first dose of heroin created that insecure feeling, and that all the subsequent doses do is to ensure that addicts suffer that awful feeling for the rest of their lives until it kills them.

SMOKERS ARE IN EXACTLY THE SAME POSITION!

Earlier I stated that the second puff only *partially* relieves the empty, insecure feeling that the first puff creates. This is because nicotine is not only a drug but a powerful poison. Our immune systems build up a resistance to drugs and poisons. In fact, when we are learning to smoke, what we are really trying to achieve is to be able to inhale the nicotine from the particular brand of cigarette that we smoke without coughing or finding it offensive. After just a short period of smoking, providing we persevere, we become immune to the foul taste and smell.

But as we build immunity to the drug, we don't quite get back to the feeling of confidence and relaxation that we had before we took the first shot. Now, you would expect that with a pastime as unhealthy, lethal, disgusting and expensive as smoking, the natural tendency would be to smoke less and less. However, we all know that the reality is the complete opposite; the more the drug drags you down, the greater the illusion of dependence and the greater the intake.

I describe my method of helping smokers to quit as 'THE EASY WAY TO STOP SMOKING'. This is because it is actually easy for any smoker to quit provided they completely understand the nature of the nicotine trap. However, it is not necessarily easy to help every individual smoker realize that it is easy to quit. At our clinics it takes approximately 4 hours for the majority of smokers to realize this. Unfortunately there are some that we fail to convince.

We are in a similar situation here. This book is entitled: 'How to Stop Your Child Smoking'. Nobody knows better than me how difficult it is to persuade youngsters to quit once they are hooked. Nobody knows better than me how easy it is for youngsters to get hooked.

I can't tell you how frustrating I find it when I go

jogging in the mornings and see that group of young schoolgirls puffing away as if it's the greatest thing in the world. If only I could explain to them. Whether I like it or not I do not have the opportunity. I've no doubt that you would like me to do it for you. Unless someone gives me enough time on national TV I'm not able to do that. But you are. You might find it difficult to communicate with your children. But with the situation as it is, this is the only hope they have. I have the knowledge to do it but not the means. The Government has the means but not the knowledge. Teachers have neither the means nor the knowledge.

Your children are dependent upon you and between us we can make it easy for them to avoid getting hooked on drugs. With my experience at the girls' school mentioned in Chapter 3, how could I be hopeful that it is possible for youngsters to avoid the drugs trap throughout their lives? I must confess that experiences like that have at times caused me to despair and wonder if I'm fighting a losing battle.

But that experience also gave me great hope. Those girls didn't laugh me off the stage as an old fogey. I was impressed by their attitude and their maturity. They listened to what I had to say. The teacher who invited me informed me that several of the girls decided to quit as a result of my visit. I don't know what percentage of them actually quit. Perhaps it was only a comparative few. But bear in mind that I was a lone voice giving them a perspective about drug addiction that they had not considered before. Just think how more potent that perspective will be when they hear it from their parents and their peers.

Do you believe that if it were possible for us to communicate with flies, that even if the fly had only a tenth of the intelligence that our children have, we couldn't explain to the fly the subtleties of the pitcher-plant trap, so that the fly could avoid falling into it?

Why do our children keep falling for the drug trap? Because the authorities themselves don't understand the nature of the trap. They rely on telling youngsters that drugs can be dangerous or even lethal. That's like telling youngsters that motor-bikes can be dangerous and lethal. The nicotine trap is exactly the same today as the day I fell into it.

We are aware that cigarette smoking can cause lung cancer and other horrendous diseases. We are equally aware that one cigarette won't do that. Therefore there is no fear of trying just one cigarette. That first cigarette tastes awful and any fear we might have had about becoming hooked has been removed. We are already hooked, yet another victim of that ingenious, subtle trap.

In order to help your child avoid falling into the trap you need to understand the exact nature of the trap yourself. It is therefore essential for you to realize that there are no advantages whatsoever to smoking. By this, I do not mean that the disadvantages of being a smoker far outweigh the advantages. I mean the whole activity is like banging your head against a brick wall in order to get the pleasure of stopping.

I have gone to some considerable lengths to explain

why this is so. However, the whole object of this book is not to help *you* to stop smoking, but to enable you to help your child to avoid falling into the nicotine trap. If you feel that you do not completely understand the nature of the nicotine trap yourself, there is no way that you are going to be able to explain it to your child. Therefore, before proceeding, you should read Allen Carr's *Easy Way to Stop Smoking*, and if you still have doubts, read *The Only Way to Stop Smoking Permanently*.

I've described the nicotine trap as the most ingenious confidence trick that man and nature have combined to lay and how youngsters are lured into the trap. Let's now examine:

THE SUBTLETIES THAT KEEP THE SMOKER HOOKED

6 The Subtleties That Keep the Smoker Hooked

Most parents cannot understand why their children get hooked on nicotine and other drugs. However, when you fully understand the incredible ingenuity of the nicotine trap, the miracle to me is that so many of them manage to avoid it.

I have explained why, if you smoke a second cigarette, you are already hooked. However, if as a non-smoker you are regularly subjected to passive smoking, the worst aspect isn't that you are inhaling dangerous toxins, you are also inhaling nicotine and your body also suffers nicotine withdrawal. In the old days when practically every lounge, cinema, pub, bus, restaurant, etc. contained a fall-out cloud of tobacco smoke, youngsters were being groomed to smoke even before they tried the first cigarette. It's little wonder that 80 per cent of the population at one time fell into the trap.

Many parents suffer the illusion that if their children can survive their teens without getting hooked they'll be safe for life. At our clinics, we are regularly consulted by smokers who started smoking in their 30s, 40s or even 50s. The majority of these cases got hooked at a time when they were subjected to heavy passive smoking, usually at work and particularly if they worked in pubs, casinos, night-clubs or other places where smoking is rife.

The authorities tend to blame the high incidence of teenage smoking on the following influences in the order given:

TOBACCCO ADVERTISING
PARENTAL EXAMPLE
PEER PRESSURE

Although passive smoking has received much publicity in recent years, it has been purely from the viewpoint of the right of non-smokers to breathe air unpolluted by tobacco fumes. They seem oblivious to the fact that the reason why nicotine addiction is more contagious than the common cold is that you don't need to smoke tobacco to become hooked, you can become hooked by being regularly subjected to passive smoking.

What else explains why somebody who has resisted the effects of advertising, parental example and peer pressure for over 50 years suddenly finds the need to light a cigarette? What else explains why it is at social occasions, when the nicotine fall-out is at its height, that ex-smokers who have abstained for years find the temptation to smoke just one cigarette irresistible and end up in the pit again?

I would suggest that the correct sequence of the factors that induce our children to become hooked on nicotine in order of what is more influential is the complete opposite to the list above. I'm convinced the most powerful is the inhalation of nicotine itself, whether it be by smoking, passive smoking or a combination of both.

For many years I believed that peer pressure was the most powerful influence in getting youngsters hooked. Whilst it obviously has an influence, I now believe this is mainly because it is your friends that are more likely to give you that first cigarette rather than peer pressure itself. The vast majority of non-smokers, no matter what their age, see smoking as a rather smelly, filthy, expensive, unhealthy and ridiculous habit. They tend to see smokers in the same light. I can clearly remember seeing my father in that light even though I respected and admired him in other ways. I can also clearly remember, far from envying them, feeling sorry for my teenage peers that smoked. That is, before I became hooked myself. Only when I became hooked myself did I see my smoking peers in a different light.

I wonder which was the correct perception? The one I have now and had before I fell into the trap, or the one that I had when both my brain and body were possessed by that insidious drug? If I need to answer that question, we are wasting each other's time.

I've already explained why parental example has little or no effect on whether children smoke or not. However, it would not surprise me if it were statistically proven that the children of non-smoking parents were less likely to get hooked than those of smoking parents. But the reason would be, not so much parental example, but that those children had not been subjected to the same level of nicotine fall-out as the children of smoking parents have.

One statistic I sincerely hope you will help me to prove is that the children of parents who have taken the trouble to read, absorb and follow the instructions in this book are infinitely less likely to fall for the nicotine trap or the trap of any other drug addiction than the children of parents who haven't taken that trouble.

I'm aware that you might well dispute the statement that I am about to make, but, much as I am loath to agree with any proclamations made by the tobacco industry, I'm convinced that tobacco advertising has no influence whatsoever in persuading youngsters, or adults for that matter, to get hooked, any more than the latest advert that 'X' brand washing powder will wash cleaner and whiter than any other brand will persuade your child to rush out and buy a packet of 'X' brand.

The tobacco industry claims that its advertising objective is to persuade smokers who are already addicted to nicotine to buy their brand. Of course they wouldn't describe it that way. They would say: 'You'll get more satisfaction or pleasure from our brand.' The point I'm making is that you cannot persuade somebody to become a drug addict. Imagine that we were surrounded by massive hoardings describing how one brand of heroin was far superior to another. Would that make you rush out and buy that brand of heroin? Of course not, but it might well persuade a heroin addict to do so. Or let's go back to the washing powder: if your child was already washing her own clothes and wasn't happy with the results, then he or she might be persuaded to try brand 'X'.

Not only does tobacco advertising not help to get youngsters hooked, I'm convinced that it actually helps to prevent them from getting hooked. Our children might be young, but that doesn't mean that they are stupid or unintelligent. They've been brought up in a world of high-pressure advertising, they'll have built up a natural resistance to it, just as we have. They'll no more believe that brand 'X' washes whiter, just because the adverts says it will, than you or I would. They are just as aware as you or I of the true motives of tobacco advertising and will build up a natural rebellion against it.

You might well be asking yourself: 'What has all this to do with helping my child not to get hooked? If it isn't tobacco advertising that gets youngsters hooked, then why waste time talking about it? Why don't you tell me exactly what I need to do to prevent my child from becoming hooked?'

In order to answer that question we need to go back to the comparatively recent history of smoking. When I was a boy smoking was widely regarded by the majority of Western society as an accepted sociable habit that gave pleasure, relaxation and confidence. At the same time it was also regarded as unhealthy and slightly disgusting. However, the vast majority of adults were smokers and non-smokers were generally regarded as being slightly peculiar, if not unsociable. They had a similar effect to the vicar turning up on your stag night.

Then came a dramatic announcement. Smoking was more than just generally unhealthy, there was a strong association between smoking and the incidence of lung cancer. Many smokers quit at that time but the majority persisted. In any event, it seemed unlikely that any non-smokers would actually start from that point on, but amazingly, they did.

In spite of this, the percentage of adult smokers gradually diminished to the point where non-smokers were now in the majority. At the time this situation passed unnoticed, but the effect on the tobacco industry was drastic.

SMOKING WAS NOW REGARDED AS UNSOCIABLE

Bear in mind that smoking itself hadn't changed one iota. It was only society's knowledge or perception of smoking that was changing.

Many of the thousands of smokers that my method has helped to free from this tyranny have kindly credited me with being a major contributor to this change. It is a credit that I would be happy to accept were it true.

Let us be quite clear. It is possible that I can persuade a smoker to want to quit. But I cannot press-gang smokers to attend my clinics. Even if I did, the very first thing that they would do when they left my clinic would be to light a cigarette.

I cannot claim credit for creating the desire of millions of smokers to quit. What I can claim credit for is discovering a method that will enable any smoker, once he or she has decided to quit, to achieve that object easily and permanently.

However, this book is mainly devoted to two entirely different problems. The first is to prevent youngsters from getting hooked. But why should youngsters attend a clinic or read a book about a problem that they are convinced they could never suffer from anyway? You can persuade youngsters to have anti-malaria injections if they are holidaying in mosquito-infected climes. That's because they have no control over whether the mosquito bites them or not. But with drug addiction, they are in control. Why should they need protection from a situation that they are convinced they won't get into anyway?

For example, if you are going to Niagara Falls, would you feel it necessary to undergo a course which would prevent you from resisting the urge to jump over the Falls?

The second problem this book is devoted to is that of youngsters who are already hooked but don't yet realize it. They are an even harder group to reach than the ones who haven't yet become hooked. At least the ones who haven't yet become hooked don't have that little nicotine saboteur inside their bodies trying to contradict everything I say. Since they haven't the slightest desire to quit – on the contrary, they have powerful reasons to wish to continue to smoke – why should they be bothered listening to an old fogey like me, or you for that matter?

The point that I am making is this: the facts that make adult smokers want to quit do not make youngsters want to quit, nor do they prevent youngsters from getting hooked. That is a pity, but let us at least accept that this is so. Millions of pounds and thousands of hours have been wasted by well-meaning people in attempting to prevent young people from getting hooked or persuading those who have become hooked to quit. Again, if those tactics had been successful, I would not have the need to write this book nor you to read it. So let us accept the simple, unarguable fact that those tactics have failed.

Now, let us suppose that I can convince you, and you in turn can persuade your children either not to get hooked in the first place, or to quit if they are already hooked. That would be marvellous. But supposing I failed to convince you, or you failed to persuade them? Wouldn't it be so much easier if the millions of pounds and hours of effort expended on removing obstacles that made not the slightest difference in the first place were directed to removing the actual factors that got your children hooked initially or that prevented their escape?

Smokers warn their children not to get hooked. At the same time those children are being bombarded daily by those very same smokers telling them how cigarettes help you to relax and concentrate and help to relieve boredom and stress. Is it really surprising that most of us will eventually try one? A whole lifetime is an awful long time never to try just one cigarette, especially when we've been brainwashed to believe in all the marvellous advantages smoking gives. OK, we've been equally brainwashed about the horrendous diseases, but one cigarette won't harm you.

When you try anything for the first time, you

are merely experimenting. Depending on that first experience, you will decide if you wish to repeat the exercise. In the case of smoking, that first cigarette tastes awful. So why should we even want to repeat the exercise? Because we now have a little nicotine monster inside our body, identical to a hunger for food, and we need to feed that monster. We don't have to worry about getting hooked. Smokers only get hooked if they enjoy smoking, and this second cigarette tastes just as foul as the first.

Another clever subtlety of the trap is that the process of trapping the smoker is so slow and gradual that we aren't aware that it is happening to us. It's a bit like growing old. We see the same face in the mirror every day. It's not until we look at a photograph taken 10 years earlier that the ageing process is apparent. Even then we cannot accept the situation. We don't say: 'Gosh, don't I look old now?' but rather: 'Didn't I look young then?' I think one of the nice things about nature is that the general ageing process softens the blow.

However, the gradual process of imperceptibly sinking deeper and deeper into the pit of drug addiction does us no favours. Because in the early days the empty, insecure feeling of craving nicotine is so imperceptible and because to begin with our cigarettes are few and far between. We are not even aware that it's happening to us. We regard that imperceptible empty, insecure feeling as normal.

We refuse to see that we have now moved on from just accepting the cigarettes that our smoking friends seemed only too happy to provide us with, to actually asking for them. Now our friends don't seem quite so keen to provide. Now we start actually to pay good money for cigarettes – something we promised ourselves we would never be stupid enough to do. In no time at all we are not only buying them, we've got to have them; even the thought of not having cigarettes on them will drive most smokers into a panic.

Ask a youngster who has just started smoking why he smokes and he'll answer something like: 'I enjoy it.' It's quite obvious to you that he's not enjoying it. He daren't inhale and looks so awkward. The conversation will proceed something like:

Q: What is it that you are actually enjoying?
A: It gives me a buzz.
Q: What do you mean by a buzz?
A: It makes me feel giddy.

Point out that he could get the same effect by merely twisting round in circles and he'll have no answer. Ask the same youngster a few weeks later why he smokes and he can now genuinely tell you that he enjoys smoking. He won't be able to tell you why. What he really means is that he can now inhale and look the part without feeling dizzy.

Ask the same question a few months later and he'll tell you that it relaxes him, helps him to concentrate and relieves boredom and stress. He will have forgotten that he had no need or desire to smoke before he tried that first awful cigarette, nor will he question that the same cigarettes now taste and smell good and provide all these other contradictory advantages.

The trap is also ingenious. Why should he even want to stop smoking at this stage? His intake is still comparatively low. He can afford to smoke. He can keep up with his non-smoking friends. No way is it affecting his health and if it did he would give up just like that.

Imagine the physical craving for nicotine as a permanent, almost imperceptible itch. If you have an itch, the natural tendency is to scratch it. In terms of nicotine addiction that means light a cigarette. But that cigarette will only give partial relief, and even that is only temporary. It's not genuine relief; on the contrary, the first cigarette started the itch and all the remainder do is perpetuate it until the nicotine chain is broken.

Now, you would think that with an unhealthy, filthy, expensive pastime like smoking, the natural tendency would be to smoke less and less. However, it is an unarguable fact that with any drug addiction, the tendency is to want stronger and more frequent doses of the drug. It's logical really: as your body becomes immune to the drug, the less it relieves the withdrawal pangs and the greater the illusory need for it.

In fact the natural tendency is to chain-smoke. All that prevents any smoker from becoming a chain-smoker are the disadvantages on the other side of the tug-of-war, like the fear of contracting lung cancer. Some smokers can't afford to chain-smoke. Others aren't allowed to smoke at work and many hate being smokers and spend their whole lives disciplining themselves not to smoke in the bedroom, or before breakfast, or in their new car, or outdoors, or in the company of non-smokers, their parents or their children.

As the smoker's body becomes more and more immune to the drug, and the more it begins to destroy the smoker, not only physically, but by impairing his confidence and nervous system, so he is less able to resist the interval between each cigarette and falls deeper and deeper into that bottomless pit.

By now the smoker knows that he has fallen into an evil trap, and at various times something will trigger off an attempt to quit. The usual reasons are: in the early days – shortage of money; in the later days – worries about health.

Another subtlety of the trap is that when you quit smoking you soon have more money and your health soon recovers. But you now believe that you have given up a genuine crutch or pleasure. You begin to feel deprived and sooner or later you light a cigarette.

The final subtlety not only of nicotine addiction, but of all drug addiction, is that the more the drug destroys its victim both physically and mentally, the more precious that illusory boost will appear to the addict. Can you imagine how any smoker could make the decision:

I'D RATHER HAVE MY LEGS REMOVED THAN QUIT SMOKING!

7 I'd Rather Have My Legs Removed Than Quit Smoking!

I loathe writing about this subject and I regret asking you to read it. But if you are going to help your child to avoid falling into the addiction trap, you are going to have to explain to them why any smoker could reach such a stage. In order to do that, you need to understand yourself.

Another ingenious subtlety of the trap is that it makes us block our minds to the evil side of smoking. I've already mentioned the tug-of-war that smokers experience throughout their lives. On the one side fear: smoking kills us, costs us a fortune, is filthy and disgusting and enslaves us for life. On the other side: it's our crutch, our pleasure. In fact this side is also fear.

I often have the following conversation with smokers:

Q: What is your favourite cigarette?
A: The one after a meal.
Q: How many meals have you had in your life?
A: Obviously thousands.
Q: How often can you remember actually smoking that cigarette after the meal, sitting there thinking: this really tastes gorgeous?
A: Well, obviously I can't.

Q: Would you say it's like most of the precious things in life, we tend to take them for granted and only appreciate them when we can't have them?

A: Yes, I think that sums up the situation very well.

Q: So would you agree that when we have plenty of cigarettes and are allowed to smoke, we tend to take them for granted?

A: I think that's true.

Q: Would you also agree that, looking back on your life, the times you actually remember are the times when you were feeling deprived because you weren't allowed to smoke after a meal, or you were feeling unsociable, or unclean because you were smoking and sitting next to a non-smoker?

A: On reflection I suppose that's true.

Q: So would you agree that when you were allowed to smoke, it didn't particularly do anything for you, and that it was only when you couldn't smoke that cigarettes appeared to be so precious?

A: I suppose that is also true.

Q: What sort of pastime is it that, when we do it, it does nothing for us, and it's only when we can't do it that it appears so precious?

A: But you could apply the same analogy to breathing.

Q: That is very astute. Do you mind if we test it out?

A: Of course not.

Q: Can you hold your breath for a minute?

A: I'll try.

Q: Well done. Was that pleasant?

A: It wasn't too bad.

Q: But was it nice to be able to breathe again?

A: Of course.

Q: Now, would you mind lighting a cigarette, taking six deep drags, concentrating on the taste and smell and tell me what wonderful pleasure you are experiencing that I am missing.

Invariably before he has even taken three drags the smoker will reply: 'Nothing, it tastes horrible.' The analogy with breathing seems to be the same, but in fact it's the complete opposite. Of course we take breathing for granted. Of course we only appreciate the need for oxygen if we are being deprived of it. But oxygen is life. We cannot survive without it. Of course we take smoking for granted when we are allowed to do it, and we only feel deprived when we aren't allowed to do it. But nicotine is poison, smoking is death.

Smokers only assume that they enjoy smoking because they are miserable when they aren't allowed to smoke. That misery reaches its height when they are attempting to quit using the willpower method.

Something triggers off an attempt to quit. The smoker works out all the advantages and disadvantages of being a smoker and discovers what he always knew anyway – that the disadvantages far outweigh the advantages. However, the moment he abstains, the reasons that made him want to quit begin to lose their effect. At the same time that little nicotine monster hasn't had its fix. The feeling is so imperceptible that the smoker only knows it as: 'I want a cigarette.' But this creates great confusion.

He has worked out massive reasons why he shouldn't want a cigarette, yet for some unknown reason he still does. He now feels miserable and deprived and like a dripping tap his resistance begins to wane. He begins to question his decision and eventually finds some excuse to start smoking again.

So the other side of the tug-of-war isn't really: 'Smoking is a pleasure and/or a crutch.' But rather: 'How can I enjoy life or cope with stress without it? Have I got to go through an indeterminable period of misery in order to get free? Once hooked, can you ever be completely free?' That is the fear that keeps so many smokers hooked throughout their lives. As smokers, it never seems to occur to us that both sets of fear are caused by the cigarette. Non-smokers don't panic or feel miserable because they aren't allowed to smoke, on the contrary they would panic and feel miserable if they had to.

Why is it that smokers and other drug addicts, no matter how intelligent, rational and strong-willed they may be in other ways, seem unable to apply an ounce of rationality to their own addiction?

During the salmonella scare, most of us stopped eating eggs. Many stopped using mayonnaise. Yet only a handful of people died from salmonella. Eggs taste much better than tobacco. Over 2,000 die every week as a direct result of smoking. Why do over 15 million continue to go through the misery?

Because the fear of contracting lung cancer is a fear of tomorrow – I've got away with it up till now and it might never happen. But if I try to quit smoking, I'm going to have to go through the misery today, and how long will I have to go through it? We've all heard of people who haven't smoked for years but still crave cigarettes. And of course the time is never right, there is always some celebration or stressful situation that we are currently experiencing or will be in the not too distant future.

So another subtlety of the nicotine trap is that it is designed to make smokers put off the evil day, to block their minds to all the evils of smoking and find any flimsy excuse to continue. This is why over 99 per cent of the cigarettes that are smoked are smoked subconsciously. If every time a smoker inhaled a cigarette, he had to be conscious of the cancerous fumes invading his lungs, that he was going to have to spend £40,000 in his lifetime on cigarettes and that this particular cigarette might just be the one to trigger off cancer, even the illusion of enjoyment would disappear. Even when we try to block our minds to the bad side, we still feel stupid; if we had to be conscious of it every time we lit up it would be intolerable.

Incidentally, you might question why I'm discussing the health aspect when I've already claimed that telling youngsters that smoking kills will not prevent them from getting hooked. That is true, just as you wouldn't stop flies being lured to a pitcher-plant by telling them that the plant will eat them. However, if you can first explain to the fly the mechanics of the trap, the fact that the plant will eat it is a powerful incentive not to put the theory to the test.

Another ingenuity of the nicotine trap is that it is designed to overcome each obstacle as it arises. A youngster will say: 'No way would I actually pay good money for them!'

But it's not long before he is not only buying them, but doing so every day: 'If I couldn't afford to smoke I'd quit.'

Don't worry, you'll always be able to afford cigarettes. The ingenuity of the trap will make sure of that. You might go without food, your children might not have new clothes, but whether a beggar or unemployed, a smoker can always afford to smoke.

'If it began to affect my health I'd definitely quit!'

Have you taken a good look in the mirror lately? Why do you think your chest is wheezing?

I'd heard these stories about smokers having their legs removed rather than quit. I never really believed them, just as many of us refused to believe that smoking was the major cause of lung cancer when the connection was first established. Even today, when the statistical evidence is irrefutable, some smokers still refuse to accept the facts.

It's not difficult for smokers to block their minds to lung cancer. We can adopt the attitude that you are prepared to take the risk. But supposing there were some way to be certain that the very next cigarette you smoked would actually be the one to trigger off cancer in your lungs. Do you think smokers would actually smoke the next cigarette? Perhaps you are in doubt about the answer. Supposing you knew for certain that the next plane you get on was going to crash. Would you get on it? No way!

So how can any smoker fail to quit after a doctor has said to them: 'If you don't stop, you will lose your toes.' Surely no smoker would rather lose their toes than stop smoking? However, perhaps they might think that the doctor was just bluffing in an attempt to frighten them into stopping. So they don't stop, and they lose their toes.

The doctor now says: 'You haven't stopped, and unless you do, you'll lose your feet and possibly your legs.' Have you seen those films where a passenger is trapped by the legs on a sinking ship, and the only way to prevent him from drowning is to amputate his legs? I cannot watch those films. I cannot visualize anything worse than having your legs removed. Yet many smokers who find themselves in that predicament still don't stop. They now know that the doctor isn't bluffing, they've *already* lost their toes.

No doubt you are convinced that, faced with that choice, you would stop. I need you to understand why you might not. I used to believe that such smokers were isolated, fanatical cranks. Why didn't it even dawn on me that I was already one of those cranks? I was already expecting to lose my life, not to mention my legs, yet I still hadn't stopped. This is another subtle characteristic of all drug addiction. You become aware that it is destroying you physically. What you aren't aware of is that it is also destroying your nervous system, your confidence and your courage; on the contrary, you have been fooled into believing that the drug is your crutch. The more it drags you down both mentally and physically, the more you rely on that illusory crutch. Eventually you reach the stage where your life becomes so miserable that your attitude becomes: 'If this is the quality of my life with my crutch, I don't think life would be bearable without it.' It doesn't occur to us that it is the illusory crutch that has made life so unbearable.

Some years ago I was fortunate enough to discover a method that will enable any smoker to find it easy to quit. That is a simple fact:

ANY SMOKER CAN FIND IT EASY TO QUIT

However, it is not always easy to enable every smoker to realize that it is easy to quit. You and I are in a very similar position. I promise you that it is easy for a child not to fall into the nicotine or any other drug trap, simply by not taking the first dose. However, with all the ignorance, brainwashing and peer pressure that prevail, it is not necessarily easy to ensure that your child is not tempted to try the first dose.

I've already referred to *Vice Versa*. How important it is for you to put yourself in the position of your child, not to be complacent and to be aware of the dangers. How important it is for you to understand completely the incredible ingenuity of the trap. That aspect in itself might not be so easy. However, your child needs to do a *Vice Versa* too. We need to make sure that your child also fully understands the nature of the trap.

You might well ask yourself what the point is of you reading the book, why not just ask your child to read it? Have you ever built a model from a kit? Did you find the instructions a necessary bore and that what you really enjoyed was the actual construction of the kit? Now, just consider how boring those instructions would be if you had no intention of building the kit. They would not only be boring but meaningless.

You have purchased this book because you fear that your child might fall into the drugs trap. Perhaps your child also has that fear. If so, that child will believe he or she has no need to read the book. They'll be convinced, as we all are before we start, that they'll never take that first dose. If they haven't got the fear, why on earth should they have any desire to read this book? Either way, it is you that needs to create that desire. I'll give more details later on the best way to go about this.

The cancer scares didn't stop me smoking. I knew smoking would kill me. With most smokers it's a case of: 'It won't happen to me or I'll quit before it does.' I was expecting it to happen every day.

However, there were other aspects on the health side which I only discovered after I quit. I honestly believe that had I known about them when I was a smoker, it would have helped me to quit. I'm absolutely certain that had I known about them before I lit the first cigarette, I would never have lit it. Perhaps it will help your child to avoid lighting that first cigarette by knowing:

THE WAY SMOKING AFFECTS YOUR HEALTH

I am not trying to under-play the effects of diseases like lung cancer, heart disease, arteriosclerosis, emphysema, angina, thrombosis, bronchitis and asthma. They are terrible and it is an unpardonable crime that even today our society needlessly forces millions of smokers to suffer protracted, painful and premature deaths because of them, but the fact remains that shock treatment, for the reasons that I have explained, just doesn't work.

I knew my permanent cough and frequent attacks of bronchitis and asthma were directly due to smoking. But I could cope with those, they weren't going to kill me. I regarded the killer diseases, like arteriosclerosis, lung cancer, heart disease, emphysema, angina and thrombosis as hit-or-miss affairs. In other words, provided we don't actually contract one of them, we get away with it completely.

However, I'm convinced that if I could have seen what was happening inside my body, I would not have continued to smoke. I am now referring to this regular and progressive gunging up of our circulatory system. It wouldn't be quite so bad if we just starved every cell in our bodies of oxygen and other nutrients, but we actually replace that shortage with numerous poisonous compounds such as nicotine, carbon monoxide, tars and many others.

It's bad enough that this starvation process causes shortage of breath and a feeling of lethargy, but its most serious effect is that it prevents every organ and muscle of our bodies from operating efficiently. It has a similar effect to AIDS. It gradually destroys our immune system.

A strong, healthy body is equipped to fight disease. Our most formidable weapon in the battle against disease is our immune system. The great damage that smoking does to our health isn't in directly causing diseases, but preventing our immune system from functioning properly to conquer them.

Many doctors are now relating all sorts of diseases to smoking, including diabetes, cervical cancer and breast cancer. Several of the adverse effects that smoking had on my health, some of which I had been suffering from for years, did not become apparent to me until many years after I had quit.

While I was busy despising idiots and cranks who were having multiple by-pass operations or having their legs removed, it didn't even occur to me that for years I was suffering from arteriosclerosis myself. My permanently grey complexion I attributed to my natural colouring or to lack of the outdoors. It never occurred to me that it was really due to the blocking up of my capillaries. I had varicose veins in my 30s which have miraculously disappeared since I stopped smoking. I reached the stage about 5 years before I stopped when every night I would have this weird sensation in my legs. It wasn't a sharp pain or like pins and needles, just a sort of restless feeling. I would get my wife to massage my legs every night. It didn't occur to me until at least a year after I had stopped that I no longer needed the massage.

About 2 years before I quit, I would occasionally get violent pains in my chest, which I feared must be lung cancer but now assume to have been angina. I haven't had a single attack since I quit.

When I was a child I would bleed profusely from cuts. This frightened me. No one explained to me that bleeding was in fact a natural and essential healing process and that the blood would clot when its healing purpose was completed. I suspected that I was a haemophiliac and feared that I might bleed to death. Later in life I would sustain quite deep cuts yet hardly bled at all. This brownish-red gunge would ooze from the cut.

The colour worried me. I knew that blood was meant to be bright red and I assumed that I had some sort of blood disease. However, I was pleased about the consistency which meant that I no longer bled profusely. Not until after I had stopped smoking did I learn that smoking coagulated the blood and that the brownish colour was due to lack of oxygen. I was ignorant of the effect at the time, but in hindsight, it was this effect that smoking was having on my health that most fills me with horror. When I think of my poor heart trying to pump that gunge around restricted blood vessels, day in and day out, without missing a single beat, I find it a miracle that I didn't suffer a stroke or a heart attack. It made me realize, not how fragile our bodies are, but how incredibly strong they are, provided of course that you don't systematically poison them.

I had liver spots on my hands in my 40s. In case you don't know, liver spots are those brown or white spots that very old people have on their faces and hands. I tried to ignore them, assuming that they were due to early senility caused by the hectic lifestyle that I had led. Four years after I had quit, a smoker at the Raynes Park clinic remarked that when he had stopped previously, his liver spots disappeared. I had forgotten about mine. To my amazement, they too had disappeared.

For as long as I can remember, I had spots flashing in front of my eyes if I stood up too quickly, particularly if I were in a bath. I would feel dizzy as if I were about to black out. I never related this to smoking. In fact I was convinced that it was quite normal and that everyone else experienced similar effects. Not until 5 years after I had quit did an ex-smoker tell me that he no longer had that sensation. I realized that I no longer had it either.

You might conclude that I am somewhat of a hypochondriac. I believe that I was when I was a smoker. One of the great evils about smoking is that it fools us into believing that nicotine gives us courage, when in fact it gradually and imperceptibly dissipates it. I was shocked when I heard my father say that he had no wish to live to be 50. Little did I realize that 20 years later I would have exactly the same lack of *joie de vivre*. You might conclude that this chapter has been one of necessary, or unnecessary, doom and gloom. I promise you it is the complete opposite. I used to fear death when I was a child. I used to believe that smoking removed the fear. Perhaps it did. If so, it replaced it with something infinitely worse:

A FEAR OF LIVING

I believe we have now more than adequately explained the subtleties and nature of the nicotine trap. This knowledge alone might well prevent your child from falling into the trap. But I believe there is a much more powerful reason that will help your child to avoid the trap of drug addiction.

Compare the problem of preventing your child from smoking that first experimental cigarette with the problem of preventing weeds from infesting your lawn. It's rather like trying to eradicate a particular commercial trade – you can attempt to remove the supply of the product, or the demand, or both. You could easily solve your lawn problem by guarding the lawn day and night and removing every seed that landed.

Did I say easily? It doesn't take much imagination to realize that would be an impossibility. Yet amazingly, that is one of the major approaches that the authorities have traditionally adopted to solve the drug problem.

Make marijuana illegal, don't allow youngsters to buy cigarettes or alcohol under a certain age. Was nothing learned from the prohibition experiment? Not only did it not solve the alcohol problem, it created an infinitely worse problem – mob rule. Do we really need to experiment? Isn't it blatantly obvious that far from reducing demand, restricting supply merely increases demand? War-time rationing proved that.

The best way to keep weeds off your lawn is to prepare it in such a way that it is not receptive to weed seeds, and the best way to do that is to ensure that it is so abundant with grass that there is little room for weed seeds to germinate and thrive.

Perhaps you are wondering what this has to do with preventing your child from becoming hooked. It is very similar. The grass that makes up your lawn is itself a prolific weed. Just think how quickly it will spread on to your flower beds if unchecked. Therefore your lawn starts off with a great advantage.

Your children also start off with a great advantage in not getting hooked on drugs – all creatures on this planet instinctively know that there is something evil about breathing lethal poisons into their lungs, and all young-sters hate smoking until they become hooked themselves. However, we have also inflicted them with a huge disadvantage: far from preparing them so that their minds are not receptive to drugs, we have brainwashed them from birth to believe that they are both physically and mentally incomplete and cannot survive without them.

It frightens me nowadays that all youngsters seem to be searching for some pill or prop, as if whoever created us has omitted some important ingredient, or as if 3 billion years of evolution, far from producing the most powerful and prolific survival machine on the planet, have come up with an incomplete dud.

This void doesn't end with adolescence, it continues

through middle age into old age. We have powerful businessmen at our clinics literally trembling: 'How will I be able to answer the phone without a cigarette?' We say: 'But the phone won't bite you or blow up, your stress is caused by your illusory dependence on nicotine, non-smokers don't have this problem!'

Western society has produced a race of neurotics and hypochondriacs, convinced that they cannot survive without pills. Much of it we attribute to the terrible stresses that we are subjected to. What terrible stresses? We have eliminated most of the genuine stresses. When you leave your home, are you terrified that you will be attacked by wild animals? Are you worried where your next meal is coming from or whether you'll have a safe shelter to sleep in tonight?

Now compare our lives with that of a wild animal. A rabbit's life consists solely of survival. Even when it's in its burrow it's not safe. Yet it can procreate at a much higher rate than human beings. It can feed its family and the average rabbit looks much happier than the average human being. It is already equipped with adrenalin and all the other drugs that it needs to survive. So are we! The human species is the pinnacle of creation or natural selection. The human species has dominated this planet for hundreds of thousands of years without the need for drugs or pills.

Look at the other end of the scale. It was announced on the news just today that a survey was taken at a 'rave' and 87 per cent of the youngsters admitted they were on some sort of drug (in addition to nicotine and alcohol).

Why is it that we feel that we cannot enjoy a social occasion unless we smoke, and/or drink and/or use other chemicals?

Watch children at a birthday party. They'll arrive inhibited. Butter wouldn't melt in their mouths. Five minutes later they are wrecking the place, on a complete 'high'. They don't need nicotine, alcohol or any other external stimulants. A true high is just feeling great to be alive!

So who teaches them that they are incomplete, that they need nicotine, alcohol and other drugs either to enjoy life or to cope with it? Is it the evil pushers of tobacco, alcohol and drugs? No. They merely supply the demand that you and I create. It is Western society generally that creates this void in the minds of our youngsters and we do it in so many different ways. Let's look at some of these ways and see what we can do to negate them. We are subjected to one of the most powerful right from birth:

THE BRAINWASHING

9 *The Brainwashing*

Be you smoker, ex-smoker or non-smoker, I have no doubt that from the moment you felt that your children were capable of understanding, you have explained to them the evils and dangers of smoking and other drugs.

If you are a smoker yourself, you have completely wasted your time, and if you genuinely wish to prevent your children from becoming hooked, the first thing you must do is to quit yourself. If you are a smoker, you might well be tempted to discard this book in the waste-bin. Before you do, let me assure you that the greatest pleasure that you will obtain from quitting will be purely selfish. I promise you that you will enjoy life so much more.

An added bonus is that you will have a much greater chance of preventing your children from becoming hooked. If you continue to smoke, it is possible that they won't get hooked anyway, but it will be in spite of you not because of you. How can you possibly persuade your children to avoid the ingenuity of the nicotine trap if you don't understand it yourself?

From birth, your children have been subjected to massive brainwashing on a daily basis, telling them that cigarettes relax them, help them to concentrate, relieve boredom and stress. Every time they see a film when someone is about to be executed, what is their last request? Isn't that really saying: 'The most precious experience on this earth, the thing I most want before I die, is a cigarette?' It could also be interpreted as: 'I'm about to undergo a most terrifying experience. I can think of no better prop to help me through it than a cigarette.' Either way, can you think of a more powerful advert for a cigarette?

Every time they see a film in which a husband is waiting outside a maternity unit, he is chain-smoking. The moment the baby is born, cigars are handed out. The message is obvious: smoking helps during stressful situations and is a great way to celebrate once the tension is over.

In every film, play, television programme, the cigarette is blatantly displayed as a social prop, a sexual prop, relieving stress or boredom, assisting relaxation or con-centration, and we believe it. **EVEN NON-SMOKERS BELIEVE IT!** Their attitude is – what you have never had, you won't miss.

You could argue that our children are also being bombarded daily with the fact that smoking is unhealthy, expensive, unsociable and filthy. True, but that only applies if you get hooked, and no one ever believes they will get hooked. But whilst you continue to believe that cigarettes relieve stress or give confidence (and everyone has stress at some time in their life), what possible harm can there be in trying just one cigarette?

In a funny way, just as attempting to reduce the

supply makes cigarettes appear more appealing, so all the attempts of society to frighten or humiliate smokers off smoking, or their attempts to ban smoking in certain places, actually make it harder for smokers to quit. The arguments against smoking are so numerous, powerful and logical, and the arguments for it are so few, weak and illogical, that the smoker is left with the conclusion: 'Either I get some immense pleasure or crutch from smoking, or it holds some immense power over me, otherwise why would I do it? And why would millions of others continue to do it?'

Why indeed? Such is the ingenuity of the trap. But why shouldn't our intelligent youngsters come to the same conclusion: why would smokers spend a fortune and take the tremendous risks that they do unless they got some immense pleasure or crutch from smoking? Every time your child sees another human being light a cigarette or cigar, that person is in effect saying to your child: 'I do get pleasure and/or benefits from smoking.'

We've been brainwashed from birth to believe that smoking helps youngsters to feel like adults, that cigarettes make young men feel tough and makes young ladies feel sophisticated. Is it surprising when every top snooker or darts player was a heavy smoker? Even in more athletic sports like cricket and football, many of our heroes were heavy smokers.

Fortunately top snooker players in recent years are non-smokers. They've helped to explode the myth that cigarettes help to relax and steady the nerves. But it's no good me telling you that and you just nodding in agreement. You not only need to educate your children, you need to help me to educate the rest of society in the true facts about smoking and other drug addictions.

Society works under the misapprehension that you will help smokers to quit and prevent youngsters from becoming hooked:

BY TELLING THEM WHY THEY SHOULDN'T SMOKE

Why does it never seem to occur to these people that smokers do not smoke for the reasons that they shouldn't, and the only way to help them to quit is to:

REMOVE THE ILLUSORY REASONS THAT THEY DO?

The only way to prevent them from becoming hooked is not to advise them of all the reasons why they shouldn't light that first experimental cigarette, but to:

REMOVE THE REASONS THAT MAKE THEM LIGHT IT

All smokers know that they are mugs and our children are equally aware of the down-side of smoking. However, society still perpetuates the myth that there is some up-side, some genuine crutch or pleasure derived from smoking. It still perpetuates the myth that smoking is a habit. It still perpetuates the myth that smokers smoke because they choose to smoke.

Until we explode all these myths, our children will

never be completely safe. Every time you hear someone perpetuate these myths, whether it be an individual person giving an opinion, or a radio or TV programme, or an article in a newspaper, express your outrage! Inform your children of the true facts.

Only a few years ago the expression 'One for the road' was widely considered to be an acceptable and sociable comment to a departing guest. In just a few years, the 'No Drink – No Drive' campaign has reversed that social attitude, with the exception of a few dinosaurs.

All smokers wish they had never started. All smokers secretly want to quit. But because they feel stupid being smokers, they find it necessary to distract themselves and other people from their stupidity by trying to justify smoking.

Ironically, it is only other smokers who cause us to try that experimental cigarette in the first place. Even when we have ourselves fallen into the trap and success-fully escaped from it, it is only other smokers who make us feel we are missing out.

If only all smokers would be honest and admit that they would love to be non-smokers, the whole filthy nightmare would suffer the same death as snuff-taking in just a few years. You need to help to persuade smokers to do just that.

It's not difficult to appreciate the effect this massive daily brainwashing has on our children. It would be surprising if any of them did believe that smokers obtain no genuine pleasure or crutch from smoking. At the same time society has also brainwashed them to believe that there is a void in their lives, that they are incomplete, that they are dependent on external chemicals. The effect is:

WE BELIEVE THAT WE ARE WEAK AND VULNERABLE

10 *We Believe That We Are Weak and Vulnerable*

In Western society we treat pregnancy and birth rather like a disease. The mother has to have pre-natal and post-natal attention. The baby is cosseted and pampered as if it were the most fragile object on earth. Yet amazingly, in serious vehicle collisions or plane crashes, a baby is often the lone survivor.

Don't misunderstand me, I'm not arguing that we shouldn't pamper and protect both the mother and the child, but we must accept that the effect is to make both believe that they are weak and vulnerable.

From birth we are brainwashed to believe that we are dependent on pills and medicines. Every time we get a cold or flu, diarrhoea, indigestion, constipation, headache, stomach ache, back ache or whatever, we go rushing off to the doctor or chemist or draw from our own considerable stocks of pills and medicines. We have pills to make us sleep, pills to relax us and pills to hype us up.

Most of my life I have suffered from constipation and indigestion. I really believed that both the complaints and the incredible variety of pills and medicines that claim to cure them were quite natural.

Why didn't someone tell me at the beginning that the

human body wasn't programmed to be diseased, that constipation and indigestion are caused by eating the wrong foods and that the way to solve the problem is not to become dependent on pills, but to prevent it by eating the correct foods?

Measuring the total time that the human race has existed on this planet as one day, this dependence on pills and medicines only appeared in the last micro-second. How did our ancestors survive? How is it that wild animals survive?

Whatever you believe the rights or wrongs are, what is undeniable is that the effect of the brainwashing is to make us believe that we are physically fragile. We can't even clean our teeth without the use of scented paste, wash our bodies without scented soap, or wash our hair without scented shampoo. Many of us even feel the need to cover our bodies with powder.

It's bad enough that we've created a society of hypo-chondriacs and people who feel physically vulnerable, but one of the worst aspects of drug addiction is that many of our physically strongest specimens – our athletes – are now sacrificing their health as well, becoming cheats and ruining their sport in the belief that we are dependent on drugs.

The illusion of physical dependence is bad enough. What is worse, however, is the illusion that we are also mentally incomplete, the belief that:

WE NEED SOMETHING FOR OUR NERVES

11 *We Need Something for Our Nerves*

The human race has a considerable advantage over other species. We have intelligence, other species act mainly from instinct. However, instinct itself is the result of evolution, a process of natural selection that teaches all species how best to survive. This process of trial and error has been going on for over 3 billion years. Now, that is an incredibly long period of experimentation in order to get things working properly.

No doubt we've all experienced the humiliation of being told by our elders and betters after making what we considered to be a perfectly rational suggestion: 'Look, I've been doing this for 20 years, when you've been doing it for 20 years I'll listen to you, in the meantime, you listen to me.' Now, unless you had a good reason to think otherwise, you'd be pretty stupid to argue against someone who had 20 years of experience. Just think how incredibly stupid it would be to contradict 3 billion years of experience.

Whenever you allow your intelligence to contradict your natural instincts, you are being incredibly stupid and, paradoxically, are not acting in an intelligent way. Whenever the human race uses its powers of deduction to contradict the laws of nature, the advantage of intelligence becomes a distinct disadvantage. There are literally thousands of examples.

How do we know the difference between food and poison? Simple: our parents teach us, and until we are old enough to learn, they'll keep poisons locked up out of our reach. But have you ever considered how wild animals know the difference between food and poison?

Put yourself in the position of the Creator. You've gone to immense effort producing this incredible variety of animals – how would you ensure that they didn't poison themselves the moment they were born? I think I've got a simple yet ingenious solution to the problem. I'd provide each creature with a sense of smell and taste and I'd make poisons smell and taste awful and food smell and taste good.

Of course, this isn't really my suggestion, that is exactly what the Creator did, and a classic example of allowing our intelligence to contradict our instinct is that first cigarette. All animals, including human beings, hate the taste and smell of tobacco before they become addicted. If you wish to test it out, try blowing tobacco smoke into your pet's face. Intelligent man finds those first puffs just as offensive, that is your body saying: 'This is poison, don't touch it.' If only we'd followed our natural instinct.

We think of fear, pain and nerves as evils. On the contrary, they are all essential to our survival. Without a fear of heights, water, fire or of being attacked, we would take needless risks and not survive. Pain is your body informing you that something is wrong and telling you and your immune system to do something about it.

Some people are born feeling little or no pain. They can readily sustain great injuries. If you or I tread on a nail, the pain will immediately make us withdraw the foot; if we lean on a hot stove, we'll immediately retract. But a person who feels no pain will increase the pressure on the nail and only realize it when he tries to move his foot. He'll also continue to lean against the stove and not realize it until he can smell his flesh burning.

A classic example of the serious effects that tablets and pain-killers can have happened to me shortly after I started conducting quit-smoking clinics. I'd reached the stage when I was talking for about 10 hours a day 7 days a week in a smoke-filled room. Not surprisingly, I suffered regularly from a painful sore throat. My wife Joyce discovered some marvellous tablets which you've probably seen advertised; they work like magic, within seconds the pain would go and I could carry on talking.

But it began to dawn on me that the sore throat wasn't the disease. The disease was that I was talking too much. The sore throat was the equivalent of the flashing oil-warning light in a car. It was telling me that I was talking too much and to rest my voice. The tablets didn't cure the sore throat, they merely anaesthetized the pain. They enabled me to do the one thing I shouldn't have done, which was to go on talking. They also did something equally bad. The most powerful healing agent that any animal possesses is its immune system. By disguising the symptoms with the use of a pain-killer, I prevented the signals going to my brain which would have alerted my immune system.

Now, it doesn't take a great deal of imagination to realize that if the oil-warning light in your car starts to flash, you don't solve the problem by removing the bulb. But that is exactly what I did when I took those tablets.

You might well have formed the impression that I am advocating that you never use any pills prescribed by your doctor or a chemist. I emphasize that this is not so. Many doctors still prescribe nicotine gum or patches to help smokers to quit. I know that they actually make it harder. I'm not denying that many smokers have successfully quit with the use of such gimmicks and would attribute their success to the gum or the patch. I know that they quit in spite of the gum or patch.

What I would ask you to do before using any pills or medicines, whether they be for yourself or your children, is not just to take them because your doctor or chemist prescribed them but to enquire exactly how they work, use your common sense and rely on your natural instincts. In particular remember that pain-killers do not cure pain; always try to get to the cause of the pain and remove the cause where possible.

You might also have come to the conclusion that I am confusing two completely separate issues. What you want to know is how to prevent your children from getting hooked on evil addictive drugs like nicotine, marijuana, Ecstasy, cocaine, heroin, etc., whereas I seem to be confusing these with the genuine medical drugs that doctors prescribe.

Would that the distinction were so simple. The vast majority of the drugs that ruin the lives of our youth today were originally prescribed by the medical profession. Also remember that one of the main objects of this book is to remove the belief that there is a void, that the human mind and body is incomplete, that we have a need for outside props.

However, I think the very worst aspect of brain-washing is that we need something for our nerves. I remember one particular clinic in the early days. I was having great difficulty getting through to a lady who was convinced that she suffered from bad nerves and that smoking helped the situation. It was a very hot day and we had the door open. Suddenly the door slammed and she shot 3 feet into the air. She said: 'See how bad my nerves are?'

There was a flock of starlings feeding on my lawn. I gave the slightest of taps on the french windows. The whole flock took flight in a split second. I said: 'Do you think they have bad nerves?'

'Well, obviously they have. Why else would they have flown off so quickly?'

'Because to them that slight sound was a cat or some other predator.'

'But it wasn't a cat, there was no danger, they had no need to panic.'

'Yes they did; if one of them had calmly waited to find out whether or not it was a cat, and it *was* a cat, the bird would be dead. The nerves of the starlings weren't bad, they were good, those nerves are their protection and help them to survive. It was exactly the same when the door slammed. In fact we both jumped. That was a perfectly natural reaction, that door slamming represented an unknown threat. The only difference between us is the slamming door didn't worry me; the moment I realized there was no danger, there was no problem. But you are still nervous and twitchy, that isn't because the door slammed, that's the effect that nicotine has on its victims.'

Many doctors are now discovering that drugs like valium and librium cause more problems than they solve. These drugs have a similar effect to alcohol – they take the person's mind off their problems, but they don't cure them. When the effect of the drug has worn off, another dose is required. Because the drugs themselves are poisons, they have physical and mental side-effects and the body builds an immunity to the drug. The addict now has the original stress plus the additional physical and mental stress caused by being dependent on the drug that is supposed to be relieving the stress.

Eventually the body builds such an immunity to the drug that it ceases even to give the illusion of relieving stress. All too often the remedy is now either to administer larger and more frequent doses of the drug, or to upgrade the patient to an even more powerful and more lethal one. The whole process is an ever accelerating plunge down a bottomless pit.

Many doctors try to justify the use of such drugs by maintaining that they prevent the patient from having a nervous breakdown. Again they try to remove the symptoms. A nervous breakdown isn't a disease, on the contrary, it's a partial cure and another red warning light.

It's nature's way of saying: 'I can't cope with any more problems, stress, or responsibility. I've had it up to here. I need a rest. I need a break!'

The problem is that strong-willed, dominant people tend to take on too much responsibility. Everything is fine while they are in control and can handle it. In fact they thrive on it. However, everyone has phases in their life when a series of problems coincide. Observe politicians when they are campaigning to become President or Prime Minister. They are strong, rational, decisive and positive. They have simple solutions to all our problems. But if and when they achieve their ambition, you can hardly recognize them as the same person. Now they have the *actual* responsibility of office, they have become negative and hesitant.

No matter how weak or strong we are, we all have bad patches in our lives. What is the natural tendency at such times? It is to seek solace through our traditional crutches: ALCOHOL or TOBACCO. I said *natural* tendency. There's absolutely nothing *natural* about it! We've been brainwashed from birth to believe it. With many fallen idols, it is blatantly obvious that the chemical dependence has not only failed to help their problems, but is in itself the partial cause of their downfall. So it was with me, but I couldn't see it either.

The only answer to stress is to remove the cause of the stress. It's pointless trying to pretend that the stress doesn't exist. Whether the stress is real or mainly illusory, drugs will make the reality and the illusion worse.

I've discussed several factors whereby society

brainwashes our youngsters to believe both that physically and mentally they need some outside support and that pills and drugs can provide it. Another area where we destroy the confidence of our children is another misconception:

SCHOOL-DAYS ARE THE BEST DAYS OF YOUR LIFE

12 School-days Are the Best Days of Your Life

This is a complete misconception and you only need to read the book or see the film which I referred to earlier to explode that myth. I refer of course to *Vice Versa*.

It is an acknowledged fact that for any creature on this planet, life should get progressively less stressful. I suppose the vast majority of us would like to win the lottery. However, as far as I am concerned, the chances of winning it are so improbable as not to make the attempt worthwhile.

Yet every one of us began life winning a lottery with far greater odds. The chances of that sperm which comprises one part of you being the first to fertilize the egg that became your other part were millions to one against.

Now, we obviously don't remember the stress of that race but it must have been pretty hectic. Again, we don't remember what is probably the most stressful occasion in the majority of our lives – our birth. However, it doesn't take much imagination to visualize it: suspended for 9 months in the warmth, security and comfort of your mother's womb. No problems, just the reassuring rhythm of those heartbeats pumping nutrients, oxygen and life into your body.

Suddenly alarm bells start to ring. That comforting, warm liquid that we were suspended in drains away and we plunge headlong (if we are lucky) into this tight, black, pulsating tunnel. Do you suffer from claustrophobia? Try to imagine what it was like. When we eventually fight our way through, exhausted, covered in blood and whatever, possibly assisted by two steel clamps on our head, into a brightly neon-lighted room (can you imagine the trauma of that experience alone, never having known a world other than blackness?), our reward is to be smacked on the bottom and if we are lucky enough to have any energy or wind left, we are able to cry.

Over the next few months and years we go through an incredibly pressurized learning period: learning to feed, to control our hands, to crawl, to walk and talk, to control our bowels and bladders, to read and write and to amass an immense variety of knowledge over a weird range of subjects most of which we see no sense in learning. Childhood and adolescence are very stressful periods. Perhaps they do not compare with the stress experienced to achieve conception or birth. But just like the rabbit in Chapter 8, we are equipped to cope with that stress; at that stage and during the early stages of babyhood we are acting mainly on instinct.

But now comes what is consciously the most stressful stage of our lives, the time when we leave school and have to make our own way in the big wide world. OK, childhood and adolescence are stressful enough, but at least we had the support and protection of our parents and our teachers. Adolescence has always been a stressful time. Our bodies and minds are undergoing a meta-morphosis, youths are pimply and shy, girls are gangly. Neither sex knows whether the opposite sex will find them attractive.

But just think of the additional pressures that today's youngsters are under which the youth of my generation never had. We never lived in the shadow of the bomb, of over-population, of pollution of our food, air, rivers, lakes and oceans, of the exhaustion of the earth's natural resources, the destruction of the rain-forests and the conversion of our environment from natural green to concrete, of global warming and holes in the ozone layer. Other animals can rejoice in the sun, so did we, now we can't do it without the risk of skin cancer. We had full employment and knew that if we studied and worked hard we would reap our just rewards. Today's youth can achieve umpteen A-levels and still have to put up with a mundane job or none at all.

When I was a boy the medical world was finding cures for frightening diseases like tuberculosis, polio, malaria, etc. Nowadays we seem to be discovering dis-eases that have no cure like AIDS and the diseases that we thought we had conquered such as tuberculosis and malaria are now making a come-back.

We had standards to guide us. OK, perhaps some of them were too rigid or antiquated, but at least we knew what society expected of us. Nowadays institutions like marriage and religion are gradually crumbling. Today's youth are literally bombarded with facts about sex at a time when their bodies are ready for it but their minds haven't had time to handle it. They are bombarded with violence – purely for violence's sake.

Do we really expect them to turn overnight into physically and mentally strong, mature adults? The really surprising fact is that more of them don't take their own lives and that so many of them do grow up to be pleasant, responsible citizens. What cannot be disputed is that adolescence is a tremendously stressful period. And there is one more evil that we have bequeathed to them: a massive variety of pills and drugs that are supposed to help them to cope with the other problems that they have inherited from us. The real mystery is not why so many of them fall for the trap, but:

HOW DO SO MANY OF THEM AVOID THE TRAP?

13 How Do So Many of Them Avoid the Trap?

You will rarely find me lacking a positive answer to anything connected with drug addiction. Nevertheless, the question itself is negative. It's far easier to explain why someone actually falls into a trap than why they don't. However, the main object of this work is to prevent your child from becoming hooked, so let's list the probable reasons which prevent children from becoming hooked and see if we can't learn from them:

1. A child's natural and instinctive abhorrence of drugs is combined with its fear of becoming hooked.
   Your child is already equipped with both.
2. The anti-drugs campaigns reinforced by your own efforts.
   Again, your child has already had the benefits.
3. Personal experience of an addict and the misery that addiction causes.
   This might have a short-term effect. But it is rather like showing motorists pictures of horrendous vehicle accidents, it doesn't stop them driving permanently.
4. Not mixing with youngsters who do take the drug.
   No doubt many youngsters didn't get hooked because they were lucky enough never to mix with drug users. But

that was just luck. To try to prevent your child from mixing with drug takers is equivalent to attempting to catch all the weed seeds before they land on your lawn. If it's hard to know whether your own children are taking drugs, just think how much harder it is to know whether their friends are taking them. Remember, drug addiction knows no class, age, intelligence, race or religious barriers. Also remember that if you forbid your child to play with little Tommy, he'll move heaven and earth to play with little Tommy.

5. Not being able to afford the drug.

There is no doubt that shortage of money does prevent some youngsters from becoming nicotine addicts, alcoholics or dependent on other drugs. However, shortage of money is no guarantee that your child won't become hooked. The first experimental doses are usually free – good friends, who already suspect that they themselves are becoming hooked, don't feel quite so bad if they can persuade others to join them in the pit. Once hooked, be it on nicotine or heroin, a drug addict will beg, steal or even turn to prostitution to get the drug. In any event, keeping your children poor all their lives is hardly a suitable solution.

So examining the reasons why so many youngsters don't get hooked doesn't seem to offer much hope of guaranteeing that *your* children won't get hooked. It seems to be more a question of luck than anything else – there but for the grace of God go I. In fact it is good news. Your children also have the benefit of their natural instincts and the anti-drugs campaigns. They might have the additional luck and/or sense not to mix with drug takers as well.

If you could communicate with a fly and explain to it the incredible subtlety of the pitcher-plant trap, do you think a fly would fall for the trap? Perhaps it might if it were starving and had desperate need for some of that nectar. But if you first supplied the fly with all the nectar it ever needed, would it then fall for the trap? I very much doubt it. The most powerful instinct of any creature on this planet is **SURVIVAL**.

Now between us, you and I are going to equip your children with information that no other child who avoided the drug addiction trap had the benefit of, and these just happen to be the two most powerful pieces of information. One we have already dealt with, to explain the exact nature of the trap. How it lures its victims and fools them into believing they get some genuine benefit from the drug.

However, that alone might not prevent your child from falling into the trap; like the fly starving for lack of nectar, which might be tempted to sample a few mouthfuls and still get trapped. In the last chapter, I painted a rather gloomy picture of the state of the world that our youngsters have inherited from us. The object was neither to depress you nor to incriminate you. We were youngsters too when we took it over, just as our parents were when they took over from *their* parents. We all did our best to make a better world of it and it's easy for the likes of me in hindsight to point out the mess we've made. I sincerely hope that our children can learn from our mistakes and reverse the process.

Forget who's to blame, the morals or what we need

to do about it. Let's just accept the fact that our youngsters are labouring under tremendous pressures, they feel weak and insecure, they are desperate for some prop or pill to help them. It's no good us just politely explaining: 'Yes, I fully realize that, but drugs won't do that, they only give the illusion that they do!'

What good does it do to take away their illusion and leave them with nothing? We need to provide them with the nectar, or in this case to make them realize that they already have it. OK, our children do have enormous problems, but they are equipped to cope with them. I've referred to a rabbit whose whole life consists of survival and the fact that it is equipped with adrenalin and all the other drugs that it needs to survive. So are we! The human species is the pinnacle of creation and/or natural selection. We have dominated this planet for hundreds of thousands of years without the need of drugs and pills. We need to make our youth realize how incredibly strong they are both physically and mentally, that although they have problems, there is no void, they are already equipped to cope with them and to solve them without the use of pills and drugs.

We need to impress upon them the power and strength of:

THE INCREDIBLE MACHINE

If I asked you to hold up your left hand, you might pause for a second before deciding which hand was your left, but few would describe that as a particularly complicated feat. In fact you could train most dogs to do it. However, imagine your task was to get every one of the millions of people that inhabit the earth to hold up their left hands simultaneously. Even with modern communications your chances of success would be infinitesimal. Yet that is virtually what is happening every time you perform the simplest of tasks like subconsciously scratching your nose.

Your body is comprised of trillions of cells, each cell a separate entity, yet all working in complete cohesion with the others throughout your life. Do you think you could peel apples, read your newspaper, play cards and answer the telephone? Of course you could – none of those tasks is particularly complicated. But would you complete one of those tasks efficiently if you attempted to do them all at the same time?

We are fully aware of the incredible skills that certain human beings achieve in activities such as sports, music, sculpture, painting, etc., but those trillions of cells that make up our bodies undertake not just one simple task, but dozens of incredibly complicated tasks at one and the same time throughout our lives.

Whether you are awake or asleep, your lungs continue to breathe in oxygen and your heart continues to pump that oxygen and other chemicals through the circulatory system to the part of the body that requires them. Your internal thermostat continues to keep your body temperature at the required level. Your body continues to digest food, assimilate the necessary fuel and nutrients and process the waste products without your having to wake up in the proverbial. Your immune system fights a constant battle to overcome injury and infection.

The problem is, because these functions are automatic and require no conscious effort on our part, we tend to take them for granted. Although it is not necessary for you to understand the technical details, it is important that you are consciously aware of the incredible strength and sophistication of the human body.

But mankind did not create itself. Nor did man create a single living creature on this planet. If man did not create himself, then God or some other intelligence did. For convenience, I'll refer to that intelligence as the Creator. (Personally, I find it difficult to believe that the Creator is an old man with a long white beard, who is permanently observing and judging me.)

The fact that I refer to him in the masculine gender might imply that I believe him to be of human form and male. To me that would be about as logical as a computer that was sophisticated enough to contemplate its creator, assuming that mankind was shaped like a computer and that just one genderless human being created all computers and everything else in the universe. I refer to the Creator in the male gender because I don't know how else to refer to him. But what is blatantly obvious is that the Creator must be a million times more intelligent than mankind.

Some people believe that we are not so much the product of the Creator as of a coincidental progression from a primeval soup to our present-day sophistication through a process of evolution and natural selection. I do not see the two concepts of Creator or evolution as being in conflict. We know that the Rolls-Royce and a huge variety of other sophisticated vehicles were developed over a period of time by a process very similar to evolution and natural selection. We also know that these vehicles were not the result of coincidence, but of intelligence.

Whether or not you believe that the human body is the product of a Creator, or of 3 billion years of experimentation or a combination of the two, what is undeniable is that the human body is a million times more sophisticated than the most sophisticated computer or spacecraft that man has created. Man has made tremendous progress in the field of technology; we've learned to split the atom but we haven't the slightest idea how to create one.

The human body consists of a variety of chemicals controlled by the human brain. Drugs like adrenalin will be produced automatically as and when required. A healthy human body is complete in itself. It is sheer lunacy to believe that the Creator of a product a million times more sophisticated than anything man is capable of creating would have omitted some vital ingredient. I have absolute belief that we are equipped to handle any situation without the need of drugs or similar aids. Even if the Creator had omitted some important ingredient, for man to believe that he can correct the omission by the use of drugs is not only arrogance but rank stupidity. If your television broke down, do you think your pet gorilla could repair it? That's virtually what happens when man interferes with the chemical balance of the human body.

Every time we interfere with the natural functioning of our body without understanding the full long-term effects, we are really saying: 'I know better than the person who created me.' We are playing at being God!

If you did let a gorilla interfere with that television, it would be irreparable within half an hour. So why haven't we destroyed ourselves by playing at being God? It's no thanks to us. A man-made television is indeed a frail and sensitive machine, which a gorilla could destroy in 10 seconds. However, such is the strength and ingenuity of the human body, that even when some misguided person like me spends a small fortune system-atically poisoning it for a period of over a third of a century, that incredible machine survived in spite of my efforts.

Just take smoking as an example: the first cigarettes taste awful. That is a warning from your body. It is telling you: 'POISON! DON'T TOUCH!' Lesser unintelligent creatures would heed that warning, but the human species has been brainwashed to ignore it. Does your body just leave you to your fate? No way! Other alarms start to operate; you begin to cough, to feel nauseous, you might actually vomit. Even if you fail to heed all the warnings and continue to smoke, your body will begin to build an immunity to the poisonous effects. Rasputin was eventually able to survive a dose of arsenic 20 times greater than the dose that would kill an average human being, all because he built an immunity to the poison. Rats and mice could survive Warfarine after just 3 generations.

So sophisticated is the system that your body, suspecting that you have no choice but to continue taking the poison, even arranges for you to become oblivious to the unpleasant smell and taste. Could you conceive of a beautiful woman who has spent time and money to cleanse, perfume, groom and dress herself to perfection, finishing the whole thing off by rubbing 'Essence of horse manure' all over her body? That is the effect that smokers have on non-smokers. Fortunately most non-smokers are far too polite to appear to notice.

Then, if and when the systematic poisoning ceases, within just a few days that incredible machine will sense the fact and begin to eject the accumulated toxins from the ex-smokers' bodies, leaving them as strong as ever. **PROVIDED THEY HAVEN'T LEFT IT TOO LATE!** In spite of the overwhelming evidence to the contrary, there are still smokers today who refuse to believe that smoking affects their health. To me, the mystery is how my body was able to survive the truly massive punishment that I inflicted upon it for so many years.

You could argue that modern medicine has prolonged and improved our lives by interfering with the natural functions of our bodies. An obvious example would be prescribing insulin for diabetics. I've no argument against that. In such a case, the natural function of the body has already broken down and probably only broke down because of drugs. Many doctors are relating the incidence of diabetes to smoking. How can you expect your body to function properly if you regularly ingest junk food and other poisons such as nicotine, alcohol and other drugs?

If the natural functioning of the body has broken down, it would be far preferable to remove the cause of the break-down. However, if that is not possible, it is one thing to take drugs prescribed by a qualified medical practitioner, it is quite another to start taking unprescribed drugs when the body is functioning normally.

Like most of the really important things in life like air, food, freedom, security, good health, employment, love and friendship, when we have them we tend either to take them for granted, or to complain about their quality. It's only when we are deprived of them that we truly appreciate them. When I was a teenager I was aware of the physical power and strength of my body, but by the age of 48 it had become physically and mentally weak and frail. I was aware that my heavy smoking wasn't helping the physical side, but in my mind that was purely incidental; society had also prepared me to believe that old age was a sort of terminal disease.

I would like to refer back to a comment that I made earlier: 'It is an acknowledged fact that for any creature on this planet, life should get progressively less stressful.' Society has certainly brainwashed us to believe that the opposite is true, and in my case for so many years the opposite *was* true. I realize in hindsight that this was only so because before I achieved maturity, I fell heavily into the nicotine trap. While I smoked, I never achieved maturity. The effect of nicotine and similar addictions is to make you feel progressively insecure.

I achieved maturity shortly after I quit smoking. How do I define maturity? Feeling physically and mentally strong and adequately equipped to cope with the trials and tribulations of life and to appreciate the great joy and pleasure of just being alive. I've explained why adolescence is such a stressful time. I should imagine that 21 would be about the time we should naturally achieve maturity, provided we don't fall for the drugs trap.

Perhaps you would agree with me that the natural progression would be that our lives should improve as we get older and more experienced, but only up to a point. For many people the thought of middle age is anathema, and old age even more so. All I can tell you is that at the age of 48 I felt like an old man quite ready to accept death. Today, approaching my 63rd birthday, I feel like a young boy full of *joie de vivre*. Old age is a myth. Animals don't have this problem of counting how old they are. It doesn't matter if you are 2 or 92, it's not being young that's important, it's feeling young, and if you feel physically and mentally strong and enjoy life, what difference does it make how old you are? The Creator equipped us to cope with birth, childhood and adolescence; he also equipped us to enjoy and cope with middle and old age.

My realization of how incredibly strong both physically and mentally the human body really is, didn't just result because of the improved health and vitality I enjoyed after stopping smoking. It was more an extension of the mind-opening process. The human body is a truly incredible machine whose every natural function is to make sure that we survive, whether we like it or not.

Let's look at a few examples of what actually happens when youngsters take drugs. Doctors prescribe 'uppers' and 'downers' for their patients. Can we blame youngsters for thinking: 'Where's the harm in taking Ecstasy? It gives me energy. With two or three I can dance all night.' But that youngster wasn't meant to dance all night. Tiredness isn't an illness; like hunger or thirst, it is a flashing warning light. It is saying:

YOU NEED TO REST

That tiredness might be the result of an illness, or it might be the natural functioning of the body telling you that now is the time to rest. In either case, by popping a pill, that youngster does the complete opposite to what his Creator advises. That pill, far from solving the problem, has merely removed a vital warning light. Do you really believe that any pill can actually take the place of rest? If so, we need never sleep or rest again, all we need to do is just keep popping pills. Unfortunately, all too many youngsters, and adults for that matter, believe that the pill does solve the problem. Who can blame them if a qualified doctor has prescribed the pill? All too often pill-popping ends up with the victim sleeping permanently. It is essential to distinguish between an illness and its symptoms. Far too much modern medicine is based on removing or covering up the symptoms rather than curing the illness. Symptoms are not only vital warning lights, but are also often a vital part of the cure.

Imagine that you are an airline pilot, completely dependent on your instruments, your compass, your fuel gauge, your altimeter, etc. If your fuel gauge read zero, would you alter its calibration and happily fly on? Your body is also equipped with senses and warning lights, each one many times more sophisticated than the most modern aircraft, all designed to protect you and keep you happy, in fact all designed to achieve one object:

YOUR SURVIVAL

Start playing around with those instruments, my friend, and you might as well be flying blindfold. You might well survive for a while, but no way will you be happy and eventually you'll smash into a mountain.

It's not only that all these drugs actually achieve the opposite to the object you take them for, but they all have unpleasant side-effects – physical, mental, financial and social. What's more, those side-effects are also cumulative.

What's wrong with a drug like alcohol that, taken in moderation, will help you to lose your fears and inhibitions, that will make you feel more secure? Exactly that! Your fears and inhibitions, that feeling of insecurity were your protection and thus your security. The drug merely reverses a situation of *feeling* insecure but *being* secure, to *feeling* secure but *being* insecure.

Let's use alcohol as an example. From birth we have been brainwashed to believe that alcohol gives courage. Why else would our sailors be issued with a tot of rum before going into battle? Take two boys who are about to fight over some petty dispute. They are both on a loser to nothing. Their natural instinctive reaction is: 'I get no real benefit by inflicting serious injury on my opponent, but I'm in big trouble if he injures me.' At the same time, they mustn't appear to be cowards, so they go through this chest-puffing preamble, hoping that the other boy will back down, or that some outside influence will intervene before they actually come to blows.

However, if those boys are affected by alcohol, they lose that protective fear and two awful things happen. Each boy loses the fear of serious injury or death and is ready to fight, but even worse, each boy loses any inhibitions about the injury that he is prepared to inflict on his opponent. With normal fights, once superiority has been clearly established, the fight ends. When alcohol is involved, there are literally thousands of cases where youngsters have actually killed each other, not for any great principle or difference of opinion, but purely because they were affected by alcohol.

Exactly the same thing happens when driving. Some drivers are still stupid enough to believe that a little alcohol improves their performance. The truth is it slows down their reactions. However, at the same time it removes their fear of having an accident, and the effects the accident might have on their own health or that of their passengers, pedestrians or other road users. The overall effect is to make them feel more relaxed and competent. It's just an illusion. The actual effect is to transform a safe, responsible motorist into a lethal, suicidal killer!

Another misconception that we have been brain-washed to believe about alcohol is that it makes people happy and cheerful. The truth is that it is a chemical depressant. I cannot think of one really happy social occasion in my life when the participants looked back with nostalgia and attributed the success of the occasion to the volume or quality of the drinks. I can think of many social occasions that were a complete and utter bore, in spite of the fact that there was no restriction in the quality or quantity of the drinks. I can think of numerous occasions when a marvellous wedding or party has been completely ruined because one or more people had too much to drink.

Perhaps you still feel that drink does convey some benefit in helping certain people to overcome shyness and inhibitions. Again, look at the facts. Everyone has a brain and a mouth. Most people have a sort of check-point between the brain and the mouth. There is a rare breed that has no check-point. There's a direct connection between their brain and their mouths. A sort of verbal incontinence. Whatever thoughts enter their brains, no matter how boring, mundane, irrelevant, trivial, inaccurate, scatter-brained, insulting, ridiculous, inconsiderate or offensive they might be, they just come spurting straight out of their mouths. These people tend to be both unpopular and unhappy.

I am lucky. I do have a check-point between my brain and my mouth, but only one. This sometimes gets me into trouble. Occasionally, it lets things pass through to my mouth that it really should have blocked. Some people have two or even more check-points to ensure that they never say anything that might make them appear to be stupid, or could be possibly taken as being offensive. Alcohol has the effect of negating these check-points. We've all seen people who won't say boo to a goose when they are sober, but get a couple of drinks inside them and they'll take on the world!

Is anyone fooled by them? Do we look at them and say: 'I never realized Ted was such a dominant person'? Or do we say: 'That's just the drink talking'? If you are shy and have inhibitions and regard it as a problem, alcohol won't cure it, any more than an ostrich putting its head in the sand will remove the danger. Alcohol will just inebriate you. It won't solve your problem but merely stupefy you and make you forget about it for a while. You won't enjoy that stupefied condition – you can't, because being stupefied means you are not even aware of your senses, whether the feelings be good or bad. While you are in that state, you remain vulnerable, unprotected and with your head in the sand.

In that vulnerable state, you might be very lucky and only insult or offend a close relative or friend, or you might be less lucky and just write off your car, sustain only minor injuries or lose your licence for a few years. Why do I describe such things as lucky? Surely I mean unlucky? No, I mean lucky, because such things are bound to happen sooner or later if you are inebriated. You actually put yourself in the position of someone who's both deaf and blind. In fact you are far worse off. The deaf and blind are aware of their disabilities, and their senses of fear, touch, smell, vulnerability, compassion, decency and consideration for themselves and others become heightened to compensate. Alcohol deadens the brain, so that every one of your senses becomes incapacitated.

Then again, you might be unlucky; driving in your inebriated state, you might kill an innocent child and wake up screaming every night of your life in a cold sweat reliving a nightmare that is real. Football, our national game, has been ruined by alcohol. We taught the world to play soccer, then suffered the unbelievable indignity of being banned from competing in Europe for 8 years because of alcohol. Just think of all the evil that you have seen caused by alcohol. Can you think of a single occasion when it actually did some good? When you are inebriated, you lose all your senses, you are completely naked, defenceless, vulnerable. Do you really believe that you are happy at such times? Do you really believe that an ostrich with its head in the sand is happy?

At one time I believed that the inebriating effect of alcohol was a genuine short-term benefit to ease the effect of traumas. If your girlfriend drops you, better to go on a bender for a few days than join the Foreign Legion. If business is getting on top of you, and you just cannot afford the time to get away for that much needed holiday, what harm is there in having a few drinks in the evening to get your mind away from your problems?

However, the inebriation won't have solved your problem. It wouldn't be quite so bad if it had the same effect as a good night's sleep. That wouldn't solve your problems, but at least it would leave you more refreshed and better able to solve them. However, once the effect of the alcohol has worn off, your problem will actually be greater, because the effects of the intoxication will be to make you physically, mentally, financially and socially worse off than before. You now have even more reason to inebriate yourself and just like nicotine, the more you take the more your brain and body become immune to the poison, the more you need. The greater your intake, the greater the adverse effects, the greater your need. The rapid descent to the bottom of the pitcher plant is inevitable. It's the nature of the beast.

Surely, if you just drink for social reasons, that can't possibly do any harm? But if you start drinking purely for social reasons, the nature of that beast is that it might develop into drinking for all other sorts of reasons. In any case, do we ever really drink purely for social reasons? We may start off by only drinking at social occasions, but aren't we really taking that drink to help solve a problem? Because we feel immature, or shy, or inhibited, or because we want to be accepted as one of the crowd? If you start imbibing alcohol for purely social reasons, you run the risk of sliding down that slippery slope that can develop into what AA describe as chronic alcoholism!

THAT IS THE NATURE OF THE BEAST

But there are people who can use alcohol, nicotine, even heroin, all their lives and never become alcoholics or addicts. That is purely because through the nature of these drugs it takes many years for the majority of victims to realize that they have become dependent on them. As with smoking, the rate at which any particular individual descends to the depths of the pitcher-plant depends on many different factors, such as their physical capacity to cope with the poison, their wealth, the amount of stress in their lives, the company they keep. It is true that once on Skid Row, wealth doesn't come into it, the addict will find the money, but just as many youngsters never started smoking purely because they couldn't afford to, so many drinkers remained casual drinkers because they couldn't afford to do otherwise. Obviously, many flies die of natural causes before they reach the depths of the pitcher-plant. In the same way, many smokers, drinkers and other drug addicts quit or die before they descend to Skid Row.

Don't let the fact that many of these traps have subtle delays confuse the issue. You certainly wouldn't envy the poor mouse for the split second of euphoria between nibbling the cheese and that steel bar smashing down on his nose or neck. Would you envy a fly that had just landed on a pitcher-plant and taken its first dose of the nectar?

Perhaps you feel that we have drifted from our main objectives of how to prevent your children from becoming hooked on drugs and how to help them escape if they are already hooked. Not so. The two main factors that cause our youngsters to become hooked both result from the massive brainwashing which they are subjected to from birth:

1. That the practice of imbibing nicotine, alcohol and other drugs, though it might involve certain risks or hazards, nevertheless provides certain benefits to the user and that those benefits will outweigh the risks or hazards if the user is aware of them and remains in control.
2. That youngsters are incomplete without such chemicals.

It is absolutely essential to remove both misconceptions and you will not be able to convince your child unless you yourself are convinced.

Before concluding, I would like to deal with a couple of other aspects of smoking, and the connection between smoking, alcohol and other drug addiction. The first is:

THE PREPONDERANCE OF FEMALE SMOKERS

When I started jogging in the mornings after I finally quit smoking some 14 years ago, I was shocked by the number of small boys, 8- and 9-year-olds, puffing away as bold as brass. Gradually, over the years, they have been superseded by an even more shocking spectacle. Pat Duffy of the *Sligo Times*, who reviewed my first book, summed up the situation far better than I could:

If you happen to be in Sligo on any weekday around midday you will see some of the loveliest girls in Ireland. They are schoolgirls on their way home to lunch. And as you pass by you are bound to notice the girls' lovely clear skin and bright eyes. And seeing this your heart will rise on realizing that Ireland still produces girls as beautiful as any in the world. But if you are a keen observer you will notice something else about these lovely girls which may cause you to be concerned for their future. About 1 in 5 of them will be smoking cigarettes! This will depress you because you will know, unless you've been on another planet for the past 20 years, that cigarette smoking is the biggest single cause of the world's major killer diseases – cancer – heart disease – and strokes.

Now, it doesn't require a great imaginative effort to visualize what these cigarette-smoking girls will look like 10 years from now. By then they will probably have husbands or careers, or both. They will also have a car, children perhaps and the inevitable mortgage. Such responsibilities will weigh heavily on their minds and the nicotine intake will be increased to ease the tension. The once lovely clear skin will require ever increasing amounts of make-up to hide the blotches caused by damage to the circulatory system. The sparkle will have long gone from the once bright eyes. In all this one thing will remain the same and that will be the big myth, the myth about smoking easing tension, helping the concentration, relieving boredom and helping you to relax. Bunkum! The direct opposite is the case. Cigarette smoking is the chief cause of the problem it's said to relieve!

That was written over 10 years ago and from my own limited research in England, which produces equally lovely girls, the ratio is more like 4 out of 5 puffing away.

It is a fact that in Britain and many other Western countries, women smokers now outnumber men. It is particularly disturbing to note how many teenage girls are hooked. Many women believe that this is due to some inherent flaw in women's make-up. Just as it is essential to realize that there is no such thing as an addictive personality, it is essential to know that it is just as easy for any woman to quit as it is for any man. It is also necessary for you to understand exactly why there is currently a preponderance of female smokers.

Various reasons have been put forward by the so-called experts as to the reason for the reversal of the previous trend. Because in the old days smoking was not considered to be ladylike, there were more male smokers. Some experts maintain that the change is due to the women's lib movement: they not only have to wear trousers and take over our jobs, but they have to accentuate the point by adopting our disgusting habits. The number of female executives that find it necessary to use a preponderance of 4-lettered words might lend credence to this view. However, I do not believe that a smoker decides to become a smoker for any reason, any more than a fish decides to get hooked.

The chauvinists will tell you that it's not so much that more women smoke than men as that since smoking became anti-social, more men have succeeded in stopping. The obvious reason for this is that the stronger male has been able to exercise his greater willpower.

I'm sorry to disillusion you, chaps, but the true reason that there are more female smokers today is the complete reverse. I do believe that the women's liberation movement has indirectly been the cause. Not because the woman wants to demonstrate her masculinity, but because, although women's lib has achieved much to improve the rights and image of the modern-day woman, it has at the same time created more stress in women's lives.

Any woman executive who is holding down what was traditionally regarded as a man's job will confirm that in order to be regarded as equal to a man doing the same job, she must be 5 times as good. In TV quiz or game shows, it's still always the male that presents the show, wittily quipping away with his carefully rehearsed ad-libs. The female role is still to appear half naked, with a permanent smile, and occasionally to blurt out equally obviously rehearsed stupidities. Please do not think that I am complaining. I admire the beauty of the female body as much as the next man. But this image isn't very flattering to the female mind.

It upsets me deeply at the clinics, when we ask a woman her profession and often the reply is: 'I'm only a housewife.' ONLY a housewife! If you analyse most jobs you will discover that being a housewife is one of the few genuinely stressful ones. If a housewife has young children to care for, their very lives can depend on her vigilance. Much of her work consists of mundane tasks, but that doesn't mean that the housewife herself is unintelligent. I used to think that my job as an accountant was highly responsible. It was stressful, but only because I hated it. The job I do now is far more responsible, people's very lives are dependent on me, but I don't find it stressful, on the contrary, I thrive on it.

The main illusion about smoking is that it relieves stress. The reason that there are more female than male smokers today is because, whether you like it or not, women generally have more stress in their lives than men. Many modern-day women, in addition to the stress of having to compete with the male, still have the genuine stress of childbirth, motherhood, keeping the house clean, feeding and clothing their children. Very few modern men would be capable of doing all that, even if they were prepared to try. It's not surprising that there are more women smokers than men.

You may feel that many of the arguments that I've put forward might well cause stress in the life of a high-flying female executive, but wouldn't apply to teenagers. True, but as we have already discussed, adolescence has always been a stressful period and particularly for girls.

In the past the school curriculum for girls consisted mainly of domestic science, needlework, music and art. They were being trained to be good wives and mothers. But at least they knew where they stood. What are the ambitions of teenage girls today?

It is a fact that the institution of marriage is becoming increasingly rocky. Does a girl risk her entire future on finding the ideal partner, or is she better off enhancing her own career and becoming independent? Even if she elects for the latter and is successful, what about her maternal instincts? I'm prepared to accept that some women don't have them, but the Creator equipped the females of other species to have them and had he omitted the human species, we wouldn't have survived.

Even in my adolescent days, girls had more stress in their lives than boys. They were widely regarded as second-class citizens. They were expected to help with household chores. They had the additional physical and mental stress of menstruation. Young men were allowed to brag about their sexual progress, but if a young woman succumbed to her natural instincts she was regarded as a fallen woman and had the additional stress of the fear of pregnancy.

You might well conclude from what I have been saying that it is more difficult for females to quit smoking. Not so! All that I am saying is that, whether it's just or otherwise, women tend to have more stress in their lives than men. That being so, they are more likely to fall into the smoking trap and to remain in it. We need to spread the message:

SMOKING DOESN'T RELIEVE STRESS, IT CAUSES IT!

Indeed for most smokers not only is it the major cause of their stress, it's their nicotine addiction which causes so many other aspects of their lives to appear so stressful.

I'm not just referring to the effect that the cumulative poisoning and financial cost have on physical and mental health, energy and self-respect, although all of these factors do increase the stress in our lives, but also the panicky, empty, insecure feeling that nicotine creates. The combined effect on smokers is to transform trivial everyday set-backs, which non-smokers take in their stride, into major traumas.

Assume for a moment that cigarettes do relieve stress. You'd expect smokers to be relatively calm and laid-back compared to non-smokers. Is this the reality? Isn't it the smokers who seem to be uptight and restless, particularly when they aren't allowed to smoke? Isn't it the smokers who always need something to calm their nerves? If cigarettes do calm their nerves, why do smokers remain so nervous?

There are far too many pathetic aspects about smoking.

It is difficult to decide which is the most pathetic, but high on the list is smoking when pregnant. It infuriates me that our society makes it so easy for young girls to get hooked. We almost force them into the trap. We wait for them to become pregnant, then, at what is probably the most stressful period in their lives to date and the time when they believe they most need their little friend, we subject them to massive pressure to quit. Should they fail, we treat them with the same contempt that we would a child molester.

From the medical profession, this attitude is understandable even though it's not particularly helpful to either the mother or the unborn child. But non-smokers, ex-smokers, relatives and strangers feel obliged to pour forth their abuse. Even the girl's smoking friends will join the witch-hunt: 'I just can't understand you smoking now that you're pregnant, I'd definitely stop if it were me.' That is, until it is them; amazingly they are now able to sympathize with their friend.

Some girls are lucky. They find that just as nature alters their eating habits to benefit both mother and baby, so they just seem to lose the desire to smoke: another example of the miraculous functioning of the human body. Other girls make a conscious decision to stop, but fail. Even if the baby is born healthy, their failure, which was really no fault of their own, leaves them with a guilty conscience for the rest of their lives. Some actually succeed, then after 9 months of discomfort, fear, expectation and excitement, comes the most stressful period of their lives, the fear, pain, mental and physical exhaustion of the labour, culminating in the miracle of the birth.

If all is well with both mother and child, the fear has gone, the pain and exhaustion are momentarily forgotten. The mother is instantaneously lifted from the lowest of lows to the highest of highs. The two times in our lives that smokers' brains have been triggered to say: I NEED A CIGARETTE!

Some women who stopped for the major part of the pregnancy tell me that they lit up before the cord was cut or immediately after. Some survive the immediate impulse and are then caught out during post-natal depression. Regrettably very few stop permanently because of pregnancy. Like all reasons for stopping, once it no longer applies, neither does the desire not to smoke.

Many pregnant girls either refuse to believe the adverse effects that smoking has on their unborn child, or justify them by saying: 'I think I would do the baby more harm by attempting to stop at this stage.' Some claim that their doctor actually forbade them to stop for this reason. I could write a separate book about the statements that doctors have purportedly made about smoking. No doubt some of them are true, but I think most of them are made by smokers quoting out of context, or using poetic licence, or, another favourite ruse of the smoker, they've heard another smoker use the argument and think, if it applies to that smoker, it must also apply to me.

Now, I don't intend to go into details of the ways in which smoking can affect, injure or even kill an unborn child, partly because enough has already been written about it, but mainly because the last thing a pregnant woman wants to read about is the damage she is causing her baby. She instinctively knows that, if that was going to stop her, she would already have stopped. What all the well-intentioned people who vilify pregnant girls don't seem to realize is that the person most aware of the damage is the girl herself. She might not admit it to you, and she might try to justify her actions, but she is merely doing what all smokers do throughout their lives. She already feels guilty. The more guilty other people make her feel, the greater her need for the illusory crutch.

Apart from the pregnancy itself and the vilification that goes with it, pregnant girls are often hit by an additional shock at this time. Most smoking youngsters are convinced that they are in control and could stop if ever the need arose. Pregnancy is often the event that makes them realize that they are just another of the millions of nicotine 'junkies'.

There is one aspect of the effect smoking has on a baby's health that I do feel bound to mention. I have read that babies whose mothers are addicted to heroin will themselves suffer withdrawal pangs. This seems to be perfectly logical; after all, the same blood courses through the veins of both mother and foetus. It follows that the same principle should apply to nicotine addiction. I did a survey of the babies in my own circle of relatives and friends to find out which babies were generally contented or otherwise during the first few weeks following birth.

I freely admit that this survey only covered about 20 babies. I also admit that it was carried out on a basis that would not stand up to a scientific interrogation. A small proportion of the non-smoking mothers had discontented babies. Every one of the smoking mothers had a discontented baby!

In most cases I was relying on observations made years before the time of my survey. You might conclude that my judgement was swayed by the results that I wanted to hear. You would be wrong. In fact the conclusions seemed to contradict my beliefs, so much so that it led me to question my convictions. I maintain that the physical discomfort from nicotine withdrawal is so slight as to be hardly noticeable and that what smokers suffer when they stop, is not the almost imperceptible itch itself, but not being able to scratch it. Therefore, even if a baby were suffering physical discomfort from nicotine withdrawal, it could not possibly know that a cigarette would relieve that feeling, so why should it get unduly disturbed?

I know that when I tried to stop using the willpower method, I got very uptight because I wasn't allowed to have a cigarette. I also know that once I was aware that the empty feeling was actually being caused by the cigarette and that I knew it would soon go, it didn't bother me in the slightest. Now, I have only known those two situations: one in which I believed the cigarette relieved the empty feeling and the other in which I knew it caused it. I do not know what it is like to suffer the physical discomfort of withdrawal from nicotine without relating it to cigarettes one way or the other. So how can I judge?

There is one useful guide we can use. I have said that the physical discomfort from nicotine withdrawal is identical to a hunger for food. I don't start to cry when I get hungry, but I did when I was a baby. Babies are programmed to cry when they are hungry, therefore a baby that is suffering the physical withdrawal effects from nicotine will feel permanently hungry and will keep crying. Feeding it won't satisfy that feeling, on the contrary, the tired and confused mother will tend to overfeed it and by doing so will merely exacerbate the problem.

It's an established fact that in Western society, on average women live longer than men. However, I gather that in recent years the gap has tended to close. Is this a direct result of the relationship between smoking and longevity?

To end this chapter on a lighter note, many women attempt to quit smoking when they become pregnant and fail, but I met a woman recently who found it relatively easy to quit when she became pregnant, then got hooked again and couldn't quit. So she deliberately got pregnant again, not because she wanted another child, but because she'd find it easy to stop again. Don't try it, it didn't work.

The second aspect I would like to discuss before I conclude is:

THE RELATIONSHIP BETWEEN SMOKING, ALCOHOL AND OTHER DRUGS

We've discussed the massive brainwashing about the pleasure and advantages that smokers enjoy and how from birth our children are subjected daily to this brainwashing. We have also discussed that childhood and adolescence are genuinely stressful periods during our lives, and that although our minds and bodies are equipped to cope with that stress, we have been brainwashed to believe they are not and that we are dependent on pills and medicines.

The beautiful truth is that both sets of brainwashing are illusory. Before we start smoking, our lives are complete. By that, I don't mean that they are perfect, but that we can enjoy social occasions and cope with stress without resorting to drugs. It is only when we try those first experimental cigarettes and become addicted to nicotine that both sets of brainwashing appear to be true.

Now some awful things start to happen. Before he became hooked a youngster might have believed that he needed an outside prop, but in fact he didn't. He might also have believed that smoking might have provided that prop, but it doesn't. Now, however, he not only knows that he is incomplete, but also knows that a cigarette will fill the void. He won't understand how or why this is so, any more than we understand how or why scratching seems to remove an itch. All we know is that scratching seems to help, so we do it.

Now the youngster has a permanent void. That void is actually created by each cigarette, but the youngster believes it is an inherent weakness in himself that each cigarette is helping to relieve. His body builds a partial immunity to the poison and now when he smokes a cigarette it only partially relieves the empty, insecure feeling that the previous cigarette created. The natural tendency is to smoke more often, which merely speeds up the process until the addict is getting little or no relief whatsoever.

This is the stage when the youngster, either consciously or subconsciously, starts to search for some other chemical to help fill the void. I was lucky, I turned to over-eating rather than other drugs. Many turn to alcohol, marijuana, cocaine, heroin, whatever. They don't stop smoking, all they do is start the same downward slide into some other drug pit.

As if smoking itself wasn't disastrous enough, it is also the thin end of the wedge. It's smoking that makes us believe that we are incomplete and that chemical poisons can fill the void.

You might ask why I, who made a rapid descent from non-smoker to chain-smoker, never dabbled with other drugs apart from alcohol. I've never even smoked a joint. I believe the reason was the same as applies to some of the youngsters who never try that experimental cigarette:

they are frightened of becoming hooked. When I started smoking I didn't realize that smoking was just drug addiction, but I became completely dependent on nicotine so quickly and completely that I was terrified even to experiment with what in those days I regarded as hard drugs.

Today, whilst I haven't the slightest desire even to experiment with other drugs, I no longer fear that I would become hooked on them, so certain am I that drugs not only provide no genuine benefits or pleasures whatsoever, but do the complete opposite; I am equally so certain that my body is already equipped with all the chemicals it needs for me to enjoy life and handle stress, that if necessary I would even take heroin to prove that I couldn't get hooked. It's not the chemical reaction of the drug itself which hooks addicts, but the illusion that they cannot enjoy life or cope with life without it. Once the illusion is removed, so is the addiction.

I would only take drugs if my body failed to function properly and I failed to remove the cause of the malfunction. Even then I would only take drugs prescribed by a qualified doctor and would first find out exactly how those drugs worked. (I do take pain-killing injections for dental treatment, having stitches or similar medical treatment.)

I would beg youngsters not to experiment with any drug to prove that they couldn't get hooked. I've no need to experiment because I know that I couldn't get hooked. I'd only take heroin to prove it to someone else and I'd only do it in circumstances to prove that I understand drug addiction and if I felt it would help to win the battle against drugs.

If you need to prove to yourself that you can experiment with drugs and not get hooked, it means you do not fully understand the nature of the beast and are in great danger of becoming hooked. If you are already 'using' drugs, confident that you are in control:

YOU ARE ALREADY HOOKED – JUST ANOTHER FLY IN THE PITCHER-PLANT

Any chemical that we take must have some effect on us. That effect might be good, bad, insignificant or otherwise. Heroin is a powerful anaesthetic and as such, it has a relaxing effect on the body. However, that effect is only desirable if you believe that removing the flashing oil-warning light from your car will solve your problem. In both cases, far from solving your problem, you have exacerbated it. Even to describe the anaesthetic effect of heroin as a 'high' is erroneous, because heroin is not a stimulant but a depressant.

As I will explain in a moment, whether we become hooked or not isn't affected one iota by our first experience of the drug being pleasant or otherwise. Except, that is, if the first experience in unpleasant or insignificant, our fear of becoming hooked is removed, and if it is very unpleasant we lose the desire to repeat the experiment. By definition, it is essential to gain the confidence of the victim in order for a confidence trick to succeed. We know the dangers, so why do we take the first dose of nicotine, pot, heroin, whatever? I would suggest that 9 times out of 10, it is through curiosity, the rebel instinct, peer pressure or just sheer boredom. I would also suggest that with the exception of nicotine, the initial dose is usually taken when the victim is under the influence of alcohol.

The awful thing is that when we sample that first dose of the drug, it's not a particularly momentous occasion. After all, we little suspect that this seemingly insignificant act will soon dominate and ruin the rest of our lives, any more than the person who is about to be the victim of a fatal car accident realizes it when they commence their journey. It's only when we *have* become hooked or, more accurately, *realize* that we have become hooked, that the first experience takes on significance. Now the addicts feel pretty stupid as they look back with hindsight at that first dose. They tend to feel more stupid if they have to say: 'It was repulsive, so I went on taking it.' Far easier to say: 'I must have got some sort of buzz or pleasure from it, why else would I have continued to take it?' Why else indeed? Any addict's recollection of their first *insignificant* experience should be taken with a pinch of salt.

Most smokers believe that they only actually enjoy one or two of the cigarettes that they smoke each day. The truth is that they don't enjoy any of them. Occasionally we get smokers at the clinics who believe that they get a genuine high from every cigarette that they smoke. It's not until we insist that they smoke one consciously and ask them to explain what the actual high or pleasure is that it even occurs to them that there isn't one.

There is no doubt in my mind that it is not the great highs that keep the heroin addict hooked, any more than it is the great highs that keep smokers hooked. Heroin being an opiate, it no doubt has a similar effect as alcohol. I'm all for pain-killers used as a temporary relief for physical pain, as used by dentists or anaesthetists, but as a long-term or even medium-term solution to depression, they are merely a guarantee for its increasing.

Perhaps the real power of heroin is that it combines the properties of alcohol and nicotine. It both inebriates and causes physical aggravation through withdrawal. Perhaps you still see inebriation as some sort of advantage. But why should someone want to be inebriated? Doesn't that mean that they are not contented? That there is something missing in their lives? Inebriation merely creates temporary oblivion. In no way does it solve problems, on the contrary, it makes them worse. It wouldn't be quite so bad if you actually enjoyed the temporary oblivion. But how can you enjoy a situation when you are oblivious to it? Do you think that alcoholics are happy people? If so, just attend an AA meeting and see the reality.

If heroin does combine the dual aspects of alcohol and nicotine, they are both enormous disadvantages and double the reason never to get involved with heroin. But what we are concerned with here is to prevent your child from becoming hooked, or if already hooked, how to break the addiction. Is it the great highs or the terrible withdrawal pangs that keep addicts hooked? We have already established that you can enjoy genuine highs like Christmas without any down-side. It isn't the marvellous highs that keep heroin addicts hooked, but the awful effects of withdrawal. Let's now examine some facts about these withdrawal pangs.

Another great misconception about drug addiction in general, and heroin addiction in particular, is that the physical withdrawal effects are so severe that they will kill advanced addicts should they attempt to quit 'cold turkey'. Yet at our clinics, the worst any of these ex-addicts described it as was: 'Rather like having flu'. If you asked a thousand people: 'What is the worst experience that you have ever had in your life?' do you think even one of them would say: 'I can answer that without hesitation. It was flu'? If you asked a million people: 'You have a choice of either having flu or being a heroin addict for the rest of your life,' do you think that even one of them would plump for heroin addiction?

Perhaps you are still not convinced. Let us examine further evidence. A few years ago there was an Open University programme that pointed out how heroin and other drug addicts could serve long prison sentences, deprived of the drug they were addicted to, without any noticeable horrific physical effects. Yet when they left prison and went back to their old environment, they were soon back on the drug.

Even more remarkably, the programme described how American police posed as heroin addicts to infiltrate the system. They discovered what they were buying contained only a small proportion of heroin, in certain cases none at all. Yet the genuine addicts who were buying exactly the same concoctions appeared to be completely oblivious to the fact. If withdrawal is purely physical, how can the placebo relieve it?

The programme also briefly referred to an earlier one about an exceptionally high success rate in treating heroin addicts achieved at a monastery in Bangkok. I had seen this programme previously in more detail. At various times of the day the addicts had to drink a special concoction. The leading monk claimed that the brew would purge all traces of heroin from the addict's body. What the brew actually did was to make the addict violently sick. This wasn't really surprising as when the brew was chemically analysed, its main constituent proved to be our old friend nicotine. Isn't it amazing how nicotine always seems to be associated with other addictions, be it alcohol, marijuana, heroin or crack?

The ordeal the addicts went through was quite horrendous. When they weren't throwing up, they just lay on their bunks feeling sorry for themselves. Yet the success rate was exceptional and I believe it. The Western experts spent many hours searching for 'magic' ingredients within the concoction, mystified as to why the method was so successful. The method did help to explode the myth that advanced heroin addicts cannot go 'cold turkey'. Not only did these addicts go 'cold turkey', they were half starved and forced to imbibe regular doses of poison at the same time, yet not only did they survive, most of them succeeded in kicking their habit.

The misconception that it is physically impossible for advanced heroin addicts to go 'cold turkey' has led the so-called experts on heroin addiction, more than with any other drug, to advocate a policy of gradual withdrawal and the use of substitutes. In my book *The Only Way to Stop Smoking Permanently* I have explained why such a policy will guarantee to make success difficult if not impossible with nicotine. Exactly the same principles apply for all drugs.

I can imagine few worse traumas than being permanently blinded, but someone born blind regards that situation as normal. One of the evils of drug addiction is that the slide to ruination is so slow and gradual that the addict is not aware of it. Non-addicts will regard a chronic alcoholic, or someone injecting heroin into their veins, or a smoker permanently coughing his lungs up, with absolute horror. However, to the addict, that situation is normal. So much so, even advanced addicts aren't quite sure that they really want to stop. Heroin addicts don't get any great pleasure from heroin, any more than smokers or alcoholics do from tobacco or drink. Nor do they suffer unbearable physical pains when they abstain, any more than smokers or alcoholics do.

All that keeps any of them hooked is that when they attempt to stop, they believe that they are being deprived of a genuine crutch or pleasure. Sooner or later, they decide that the misery of being an addict is less than the misery of feeling deprived; after all, in their minds, the problem wasn't that they used the drug, but that they couldn't control the level. They don't understand that they never did control the level and that to attempt to do so only gives them the worst of all worlds – they are now both addicted and deprived.

It is in fact easy to quit all drugs. The so-called experts know that the real problem is for addicts to *stay* off the drug. They attribute this to the fact that ex-addicts return to the same environment and drug-using friends and it is this influence that sooner or later gets them hooked again. That is rather like saying that smokers got hooked again because they walked into a tobacconist's shop and enjoyed chatting with the owner. The ex-smoker walked into that shop for one reason only: TO GET THE DRUG. The reason why so many ex-drug addicts fall back into the pit is because, while they are merely being abstemious rather than cured, and while they retain a craving for the drug no matter how slight or occasional, they remain vulnerable, and because they have no great fear of the drug, eventually they succumb. They return to the old environment and seek out their old friends because they want the drug. Addicts will return to associate with people they loathe for one reason only:

TO GET THE DRUG!

The monk's method, described above, was really reverse shock treatment. Shock treatment is usually ineffective because, no matter how horrific it might be, addicts don't believe that it will happen. They can only actually experience it when it's too late. However, any addict subjected to the monk's cure survived an actual experience 10 times more horrendous than the addiction itself. No way were they going to become addicted again, because no way were they going through that cure again!

I am not advocating the monk's method, but explaining why it works. It has three major disadvantages:

1. The horrendous trauma the addicts have to go through.
2. It doesn't actually remove the basic problem of the craving, so the ex-addict remains feeling deprived and vulnerable, and some not only get hooked again, but have to go through the horror of the cure again.
3. Far from solving the mysteries of addiction, it merely adds to the overall confusion.

Fortunately, there is no need to resort to such drastic tactics. The beautiful truth is that it is easy to kick any drug once you have established that it does nothing for you at all and that you are complete without it. You might question how I can possibly group together drugs like alcohol, crack, nicotine, heroin, cocaine and the myriad of other drugs that are now on the market with all their differing effects on our minds and bodies. I do so for just that reason:

THEY *DO* HAVE AN EFFECT ON OUR MINDS AND BODIES
THAT EFFECT IS AN ADVERSE EFFECT
AND

OUR MINDS AND BODIES ARE COMPLETE
WITHOUT THEM

Before we come to my conclusions let us examine:

THE STANDARD TACTICS

17 *The Standard Tactics*

So, up to now, what tactics have our governments used to rid society of this 20th-century equivalent of the Black Death? To date there have been 6 basic approaches to the problem:

1. *Shock treatment*. Massive publicity designed to inform addicts of what they already know far better than the people who are trying to inform them: **THAT THEY ARE FOOLS!** Not only has this approach failed to cure most addicts, it doesn't even prevent our children from getting hooked.

2. *The search for suitable substitutes*. The problem is identical no matter which drug the addict feels dependent upon, but let's use smoking as an example. Consider the following conversation:

   'Why do we need a substitute?'

   'Forgive me, but that appears to be a pretty stupid question. Of course we need a substitute in order to fill the void that no longer being allowed to smoke cigarettes creates.'

   'Perhaps I'm missing the point. Normally one only searches for a substitute when the supply of the original has been exhausted. It seems to me that there is no shortage of cigarettes, so why the search for a substitute?'

'Not necessarily, a substitute might be desirable if certain aspects of the original are not really suitable.'

'You mean, although cigarettes relieve boredom and stress and assist concentration and relaxation, they are also extremely hazardous to health, expensive, anti-social and addictive.'

'Now you are beginning to understand the problem.'

'I think I see your point. You are trying to find a chemical that will relieve boredom and stress and assist concentration and relaxation, that has none of the serious side-effects of smoking.'

'Now you've got it!'

'But boredom and concentration are opposites and so are relaxing and stressful situations, do you really expect to find such a substitute?'

'It might be difficult, but we must keep trying.'

'Now who's being stupid?'

Even more stupid, the substitutes most commonly advocated actually contain the drug that the smoker is trying to abstain from. Just how stupid can these so-called experts get?

'Ah yes, you see, your real problem is that you are addicted to nicotine. Fortunately we can help you with a substitute, and you can take it either by chewing, or absorbing it through a patch on your arm, or there is now a convenient nasal spray.'

'Oh thank you doctor, by the way, what is the substitute?'

'Why, nicotine of course.'

Could you imagine a doctor saying to a youngster who smokes heroin: 'Please don't smoke it, smoking is dangerous, why don't you just inject it into a vein and wean yourself off it that way?'

The real evil of any substitute is that it convinces the addict that he or she is making a genuine sacrifice and is unable to survive without the drug. When you get rid of a bout of flu, do you search for another disease to take its place? Of course you don't! The whole key to my method is to make addicts realize that their lives were complete before they became addicted to the drug and will be again once they are freed of the physical and mental brainwashing.

3. *To alter the social and environmental conditions that make people turn to drugs*. I'm all for doing that for its own sake, but alcohol, nicotine and heroin have proved there are no social or class barriers to drug addiction. To succeed, it would be necessary to remove all forms of stress from everyone's life. A nice thought, but hardly realistic.

4. *The AA approach*. I consider this to be the worst of all in that it implies that the fault lies in the addict rather than in the drug and society's attitude towards it.

5. *To ban advertising*. I believe that this has the same disadvantages as banning the product itself. I know

in the countries in which advertising has been banned, statistics are produced to prove that consumption of tobacco has gone down. I am a chartered accountant, statistics are my stock in trade. I know just how misleading they can be, particularly when presented by the authority whose decision is being judged, and especially when that authority is comprised of civil servants or politicians. A classic example is: 'The rate of increase in inflation has gone down for the third month running.' You might be excused for thinking that was good news, especially when announced in a tone that implied that it *was* good news. It actually means that inflation has gone up for the third month running! Even if the statistics were correct and not presented in a misleading manner, how do they know it is the ban on advertising that has caused the drop in consumption? After all, there has been a considerable drop in the consumption of tobacco in the UK in recent years, but no advertising ban. The organizers of National No Smoking Day take credit for that drop without producing a shred of evidence to support their claim.

6. *To wipe out the supply of the drugs.* I call this the 'King Canute' approach: every week we hear that the authorities have busted a huge drugs ring and are winning the battle against the drug dealers, yet at the same time drug addiction is on the increase. Can we learn nothing from history? The prohibition experiment provided us with certain valuable lessons. One was that laws should reflect the opinion of society

and not the other way around, because unless they do, they will be flouted. The most important lesson was that if there's a demand for a product, there will be a supply, illegal or otherwise.

Making alcohol illegal didn't solve the problem. On the contrary, it merely created a far greater problem: organized crime. In fact the drug rings of today probably owe their success to the experience and training provided by the bootleggers. Even with heroin addiction, the authorities appear to attach more importance to the *crime* of dealing in the drug than to the misery suffered by the addicts.

Because prohibition didn't cure the alcohol problem, some so-called experts take the simplistic view that the obvious remedy is to legalize all drugs. How can they possibly overlook the fact that ending prohibition didn't solve the problem either? The two chemicals that cause death, misery and destruction a thousand times greater than all other drugs combined are both legal.

All of these things would be excusable if they solved the problem, but whether you understand why or not, they haven't. It is blatantly obvious that you cannot remove stress or depression from the whole life of a single person, let alone the entire population. It is also obvious that, while people believe that drugs will solve, or even just alleviate, their problems, they will take them, whether they be illegal, advertised, harmful or otherwise. There is only one alternative, that is to extend the solution that I have been advocating and proving to be successful for the last 14 years.

It needs a massive counter-brainwashing exercise to educate society generally, not about the awful side-effects of drug addiction, but about the aspects of drugs that are not generally known:

1. Drugs not only fail to achieve the object for which they are taken, but succeed in achieving the complete opposite.
2. We don't need the drugs in the first place. We are already perfectly equipped both to cope with life and to enjoy it.

If we can achieve that object, we have solved the problem, we have removed the desire for the drug. Any businessman will tell you that the one thing that will stop him manufacturing a product is for the demand to dry up. If that happens, he can advertise it until the cows come home, he can't even give it away.

Let's face the facts, to date we have failed even to check the rate of the expansion of drug addiction. If any of those methods worked, we would have done. The new Labour government have come up with a brilliant idea, the appointment of a 'DRUGS TZAR'. Considering the fate of the last Tzar, the choice of name is somewhat unfortunate.

But can you imagine the conversation around the ministerial meeting?

'Now, what's the next item we promised to do something about?'

'Well, this drug problem is very topical, a few

more youngsters have killed themselves with Ecstasy.'

'So why don't we do something about it?'

'It's not so easy, everything we try seems to make these drugs barons more powerful.'

'I've got it! Let's appoint some anti-drugs barons.'

'That sounds a bit corny and how many do we appoint?'

'OK, let's appoint an anti-drugs king. Then we need only appoint one.'

'That's better, but Elvis has been in the news recently, he's widely revered as the King and he could hardly be described as anti-drugs.'

'What about a drugs lord, or earl or duke? None of them has the right ring.'

'EUREKA! "DRUGS TZAR": there aren't any left, we can't offend anyone, he was all-powerful and we only need to appoint one!'

'Brilliant! Problem solved! And it was so simple – if you want a problem solved, you appoint someone to solve it.'

'Just a minute, is it really that simple, who do you appoint to solve it?'

'We've had anti-drugs specialists for years, there's bound to be some high-ranking police officer or customs officer who has years of specialized experience in drugs control.'

'But wouldn't he be an expert on the methods that have already been tried and found wanting?'

'I suppose so.'

'So how would that solve the drugs problem?'

'It wouldn't, but it will solve our problem, if he fails it will be his fault not ours, after all, he's supposed to be the specialist. We'll do what we always do, give him a knighthood then appoint someone else.'

The Conservatives must be livid that they didn't think of this simple solution. In fact they did. Some years ago I was approached by Sir Angus Ogilvy. He himself had been approached by the appropriate minister to liaise with the leading experts on the solution to the drug problem with a view to combining their efforts. During his enquiries he was advised by more than one source: 'If it's to do with drug addiction, consult Allen Carr.' He had already read *The Easy Way to Stop Smoking* and was a confirmed fan of mine. He invited me to St James's Palace to discuss the matter and explained the problem. I suggested the obvious and simple solution: 'You are an expert on raising funds. I am an expert on the only real cure to drug addiction. You raise the funds and I'll solve the problem.'

Sir Angus doubted whether he could persuade the minister that the solution was that simple. There was no doubt in my mind that he wouldn't be able to persuade him. After all, how could the solution be that simple when the combined efforts of the leading experts had failed to arrest the problem, let alone solve it? Perhaps it was because the established experts didn't really understand drug addiction and were going about it the wrong way.

In fact the Labour Party have come up with a brilliant idea. Provided they appoint me as their 'Drugs Tzar'.

The ridiculous title would be a handicap, but I've learned to conquer ridicule. There's no hope of that happening, that would mean someone having to stick their neck out and taking a gamble, or even worse, actually having to take the trouble to investigate Allen Carr's method to find out why one man can actually achieve what the efforts of the combined experts can't. That takes real initiative, real courage, far better to stick to the traditional methods that we know don't work. We can always find a scapegoat.

I'm afraid you have exactly the same problem. You too have to decide between the traditional methods that are proven failures and Allen Carr's method. It might help you to make your choice if you bear in mind that I'm famous for one reason and one reason alone:

MY METHOD WORKS

We have discussed many aspects of drug addiction in detail. My intention has been to enlighten you about the true facts of drug addiction. I hope I have succeeded. However, it is a long and complicated subject and perhaps at this stage you are somewhat confused. So let's summarize the whole situation so that we know exactly what we are trying to achieve and how best we can set about achieving it.

The primary object of this book is:

**TO PREVENT YOUR CHILDREN FROM
GETTING HOOKED ON DRUGS**

The secondary object if they are already hooked is:

TO HELP THEM ESCAPE

Let us first deal with the essentials required to achieve either object:

1. Communication

This can be very difficult. All my children now have children of their own. I have often been described as a great communicator, yet I still have difficulty in communicating with my own children. Perhaps it relates back to the time when I tried to explain to them not to cross the road, because if a car hit them it would kill them. I felt I hadn't got through to them and solved the problem by forbidding them to go near the road and making them more frightened of me than they were of the road. This technique solved the road problem and similar problems, but I suspect it created a longer-term communication problem.

Make every effort to bridge that generation gap, but if you suspect that you've failed to get through to them, persuade a sympathetic relative or friend, someone they respect, to have a go. Failing that, you can always send them to one of our clinics.

Don't lecture them or patronize. Above all be completely honest. Do not try to minimize or exaggerate the facts. Discuss the matter as you would with an adult. However, having said that, avoid this annoying penchant that some people possess of using a long word when a short one will do. In my opinion, there is only one practice which causes more irritation. No, it's not the person sitting next to you clipping their nails while you are still eating your soup. (Although I do believe that ranks third.) It is the user of the long word, assuming that you are so ignorant that you don't know the meaning of it, then explaining its meaning without you having asked for an explanation.

The fact that you hadn't a clue what it meant doesn't mollify your feelings one iota. You aren't grateful to them because they avoided embarrassing you by forcing you to admit that you didn't know what the word meant, because you weren't going to admit that you didn't know what it meant anyway. You were going to bluff it out and hope that they thought you knew what it meant. You aren't even grateful because they have avoided your need to bluff, all you are thinking is: 'If you believed I was too ignorant to understand the word, why on earth did you use it?'

The point couldn't have been better made than by the biology student who asked the professor:

'Is it true that flies take off backwards?'

'Flies take off in a certain direction, the complete opposite geographical direction on the compass to the direction in which they were travelling immediately prior to the time when they alighted, provided that is, they do not vary their direction once they have alighted.'

Understandably, there was a somewhat prolonged pause while the student and his fellow students attempted to comprehend the answer. Eventually the student said: 'Sir, could it be that the word you were desperately searching for was yes?'

Perhaps I appear to have digressed from the subject. Not so. Good communication is a skill. You won't be able to communicate with someone unless you speak their language or they speak yours. Long words do not impress people who understand them. They might well impress people who don't understand them, but they also make them feel inferior and embarrassed. This in itself will not help communication and it's pretty obvious that to convey a message by using words that the recipient doesn't understand doesn't say much for the intelligence of the sender.

When I first started running group clinics, it soon became obvious to me that the member of the group to whom my discussion was directed at any particular point was the person who least seemed able to understand the point that I was making. Logically, you would think it would be the complete opposite. After all, if my sole attention is directed to that individual, the logical conclusion is that this would be to the detriment of the other members in the group.

However, you've no doubt noticed the practice in TV quiz programmes of making the first question ridiculously easy, just to relax the contestant. All the other contestants know the answer. Every one of the studio audience knows the answer. Every viewer aged 4 to 104 knows the answer. There is only one person in the whole wide world who doesn't know the answer and that happens to be the contestant to whom the question was put. It matters not one iota that he happens to be a university professor.

It's a common phenomenon – if you're in the hot seat the mind tends to go blank. So a useful technique when approaching the subject of smoking, or other addiction, with your children, is to avoid making your points directly at them. If you do, they might form the impression that they are the defendant in the witness box under attack from the prosecutor and their defences will go up. Far better to direct your comments to youngsters, smokers or drug addicts generally. This point applies particularly if you suspect that your child is already hooked or just dabbling.

Another excellent technique when attempting to pass on information, especially when the recipient is not particularly keen to receive it, is, instead of just stating a fact, ask a question, and try to ask it as if you don't know the answer. This will force your children to get involved and really think about the subject.

Let's give an example that combines these techniques. Assume that you have just discovered that one of your children is already smoking. You have a variety of mixed emotions. You are angry, your child has failed to heed all your warnings and has been deceitful. You are disappointed. You are frightened that he might already be on his way to the bottom of the nicotine pit. All this is probably combined with a feeling of guilt that your efforts were insufficient and this guilt will be greater if you are, or have been, a smoker yourself.

One of the essential misconceptions that you need to remove in order to explain the exact nature of the nicotine trap is that he is not smoking because he chooses to, and that no smokers young or old, casual or heavy, choose to smoke. In fact, when you broach the whole subject of smoking, you might be tempted to commence with something like: 'I should inform you that, although you might think you are, you are not smoking that cigarette because you choose to.'

If that statement is delivered in a tone reflecting all those mixed emotions: anger, betrayal, disappointment, fear and guilt, you have immediately removed all hope of communication. Your child will be the accused caught red-handed and will merely react in a defensive manner without really absorbing a word you are saying. Even if he did absorb it, although your statement happens to be true, it will appear as complete nonsense. 'Of course I chose to smoke the cigarette, no one forced me.'

If possible it is better not to let your child be aware that you know he or she is smoking. Before you even commence the process, first remove those emotions, they are all counter-productive. Neither you nor your child is a criminal, the only criminal involved is that 'insidious weed' aided and abetted by a society that failed to provide you or your children with the complete facts about addiction. Start the subject with a question: 'Do you believe anybody smokes because they choose to?'

This starts off an interesting and pleasant conversation about smokers and smoking generally and gives your child ample scope to join in the conversation, without feeling pressurized or being admonished. No matter what tack the conversation takes, this will give you ample opportunity to reel off the 6 paragraphs referred to in Chapter 3.

2. Avoid the use of shock tactics

The down-side of smoking is so bad that it is difficult not to fall for the temptation of appealing to your children's common sense and hoping that this alone will prevent them from becoming hooked, or if they are already hooked, that it will make them quit.

Imagine a doctor visiting a prisoner in a camp and saying: 'Look, it's very damp here, you're bound to catch pneumonia, and you are clearly undernourished. What's more, your family are very worried about you. Why don't you be a good chap and go home?'

Such a doctor would be regarded as an idiot. What the prisoner needs, is not someone to patronize him by telling him what he already knows, but someone who will give him the key to the prison.

Now, it's not so easy to see with nicotine and other drug addicts, but they are in exactly the same position. The reason it's not so easy to see is that with the camp, we can see the barbed wire, the machine-guns and the guards. With drugs we cannot see the prison. There are no machine-guns, barbed wire or guards. So what's to prevent addicts from becoming free if we can persuade them of the stupidity of their ways?

There would be nothing if there were no prison, but addiction is a prison: **THAT IS A FACT – ACCEPT IT!**

Now, if the doctor would be stupid giving that advice to the prisoner, how much more stupid would he appear if he gave the same advice to someone who wasn't in a camp and had no intention of ever being sent to one? If your children aren't already hooked, it's just as stupid for you to hope that your telling them what they already know – the serious down-side of being a drug addict – will prevent them from getting hooked. They have no intention of becoming hooked. You are warning them of a danger that for them doesn't exist. You might just as well try to advise them what to do if they are ever bitten by the ooulong bothi snake that lives only in the south-east provinces of Sumatra, when they have no intention of visiting Sumatra, let alone being bitten by snakes of any kind.

I admit that if you don't understand the ingenious subtlety of drug addiction, it would appear to be logical to warn your children of the dangers, but if that worked, hundreds of thousands of the youth of today wouldn't still be falling into the trap:

ACCEPT THAT SIMPLE FACT!

Also accept the fact that people do not smoke or take drugs for the many and powerful reasons that they shouldn't take them, but for the illusory and even more powerful reasons that they do.

If your children are already hooked, shock treatment is equally ineffective, because they don't realize that they are hooked. They believe they are in control. They believe they are in a holiday camp, not a prison camp. If shock treatment doesn't help smokers who have already lost a limb, or who have already suffered multiple by-pass operations, asthma, bronchitis and emphysema, why should we expect it to stop smokers who have neither reached that stage nor believe they ever will?

Also remember that youngsters who have already become hooked have several distinct disadvantages over the ones that haven't. They now believe that the drug gives a genuine pleasure or crutch. They also believe that they need some chemical prop or crutch. They also have an evil saboteur inside their stomach – a little nicotine monster with an insatiable appetite.

What we must concentrate on is removing the reasons that cause our youngsters to fall for the trap. The first is to explain the ingenuity and subtlety of the trap.

3. The ingenuity and subtlety of the trap

If a fly had a tenth of the intelligence of your child and it were possible for you to communicate with it, do you believe that you could persuade it not to fall for the pitcher-plant trap? I believe you could. So, if our children are 10 times more intelligent, and we can actually communicate with them, it should be a cinch to explain the nicotine trap. However, there are some basic problems, the first of which is: why should your children be interested in the ingenuity and subtlety of the trap? If they are hooked already, they not only won't realize it, but as explained above, will have powerful reasons not to want to know about it. Equally, if they are not yet hooked they'll believe they never could be, so how do you create the interest?

I've already made one suggestion as to how to broach

the whole subject. This can be followed up with another question: 'The disadvantages of being a smoker are so obvious, not only to you and me, but to every smoker, can you explain why so many smokers did get hooked, and why even when they knew that it was killing them and doing nothing for them, they continued to smoke?' Follow up with: 'Can you imagine how any smoker would rather have his legs removed than quit smoking, even though he knows that he could keep his legs if he quit smoking?'

Now I hear you saying: 'Hang on a minute, this is shock treatment. You've just told me to avoid shock treatment.' No, it isn't. Shock treatment is when you tell your children not to smoke because they might lose their legs. This is nothing to do with them but merely asking them to observe other people. This isn't shocking but it is revealing. All you are trying to do at this stage is to get your children interested in the ingenuity and subtlety of the trap. However, it is also a subtle way of opening your children's minds to the horrors of smoking.

So, assuming you have solved the first problem, to get them interested in the ingenuity and subtlety of the trap, the next problem is to explain the mechanics of the trap. This might appear to be very simple. When I first discovered the secret, I believed it would be possible to cure any smoker in 5 minutes merely by informing them that the only reason any smoker lit the next cigarette was not because they enjoyed it, or it gave them some crutch, but to try to end the empty, insecure feeling that the previous cigarette created. What I didn't realize was that before I could get them to believe that, I needed to disprove all the brainwashing they had been subjected to since birth and explain why smoking didn't remove stress or boredom and didn't assist concentration or relaxation, why it did the exact opposite and conferred no benefit or crutch whatsoever on the smoker.

You not only need to help your children completely to understand the nature of addiction, but to appreciate that the many misconceptions about drug addiction which, even in this so-called enlightened age, are perpetuated by the media and society generally, are untrue. These misconceptions are listed in the appendix. If you have difficulty understanding any of these misconceptions, you need to read *The Easy Way to Stop Smoking* and if you still have doubts, *The Only Way to Stop Smoking Permanently*.

Having convinced your children that drugs do absolutely nothing for them, perhaps the hardest thing is to convince them that they don't need chemical props, that they have already been provided with the chemicals they need both to enjoy life and to handle stress.

4. The incredible machine

As I said before, don't minimize or exaggerate your children's problems. One of the misconceptions that you need to dispel is that it is difficult for long-term and/or heavy smokers to quit and easy for younger and/or casual smokers to quit. Like most of the facts about smoking, the truth is the exact opposite to the popular belief. The only reason why any smoker lights the next cigarette is to try to relieve the empty, insecure feeling that the first cigarette started and the previous cigarette perpetuated. That empty, insecure feeling consists of two distinct components. The first is physical and is identical to a hunger for food; it is so slight that we only know the feeling as 'I want a cigarette.' Provided we are allowed to light one, we suffer no aggravation whatsoever. The second component is also identical to food. If we feel hungry and can satisfy our hunger, the process is very pleasurable. But if we are not allowed to eat, we suffer no physical pain – OK, our stomachs might be rumbling, but that isn't physical pain; we are simply now feeling deprived and irritable.

So it is with smoking. Once we decide we want a cigarette but can't have one, we feel deprived and miserable. Just like a hunger for food – the longer we go without it, the more pleasurable it will feel when we satisfy that hunger – so it is with smoking; the longer we go without nicotine, the greater the misery we suffer, and the greater the relief appears when we are finally allowed partially to satisfy that craving.

This is why all the so-called 'special' cigarettes are always after a period of abstinence:

The one after a meal.
The first in the morning.
The one after sex.
The one after exercise.

It doesn't matter whether that period of abstinence was forced on the smoker by society or by himself. The truth is that smokers don't light cigarettes because they enjoy smoking or because they get some crutch or pleasure from it, they smoke only to try to end the empty, insecure feeling that the first cigarette started and the last one perpetuated.

It is this similarity to food that fools the drug addict. In fact they are complete opposites. Food is survival, it genuinely tastes good and genuinely satisfies hunger. OK, it doesn't satisfy it permanently, but so much the better, we can enjoy satisfying our hunger three times a day for the rest of our lives.

Whereas drugs are poisons and death, when we partially relieve the withdrawal pangs of nicotine, we're forced to breathe obnoxious fumes into our lungs. That is not a very pleasant experience. It wouldn't be quite so bad if it actually relieved the empty, insecure feeling that we were taking it for, but it doesn't. The first intake of the drug started that empty, insecure feeling and the next one just ensures that it is perpetuated for the rest of our lives.

If your children are already taking the drug, you need to make them understand exactly why they are like flies already sipping the nectar. Don't lie to them. Explain that it will require intelligence on their part to understand the true position that they are in.

Smokers and other drug addicts make the mistake of believing that they only take the drug out of habit. They think: 'At one time I was in control, I only needed to take the drug when I wanted to. But I've got into the habit of taking it regularly. If I can train my mind and body to reduce the intake or only take the drug on special occasions, my mind and body will soon adapt to that situation and I can happily control it at that level or cut down further.'

The reality is that it is not habit but drug addiction. The 'user' was never in control. It is the nature of the beast that in the early days of drug addiction, we have neither the need nor the desire to take large quantities of the drug. On the contrary, we have to force ourselves to take the filthy stuff.

It is also the nature of the beast that, as the body becomes immune to the drug, it wants more and more, not less and less. If you have a permanent itch, the natural tendency is to scratch it permanently. I used to regard my chain-smoking as a weakness. I couldn't understand how my friends could control their intake to 10 or 20 cigarettes a day. I knew that my will was stronger than theirs. It never occurred to me that the natural tendency for all smokers is to chain-smoke and that it's only the down-side on the other side of the tug-of-war that prevents all smokers from becoming chain-smokers.

You need strong lungs to be able to chain-smoke. Some of these 5-a-day smokers only smoke 5 a day because they feel sick or giddy if they try to smoke more. Some can't afford to chain-smoke and control their intake according to their pocket. Some aren't allowed to smoke at work or at home. Others despise themselves for smoking so much that they discipline themselves not to smoke in their car, in front of their children or outdoors.

You need to explain to your children that drug addiction is a continual itch that is not relieved by the next dose of the drug but was started by the first dose and will only end after the last dose.

Don't try to under-play the traumas that your children have to cope with. Sympathize with them. Help them to realize that they are going through a difficult time in their lives and at the same time help them to realize that they are fully equipped not only to cope with it, but to enjoy the challenge. Help them to realize that not only will drugs make matters worse but they are equipped with a truly incredible machine.

5. The influence of other smokers

This is another powerful influence that might persuade your children, against their better judgement, to try that first experimental cigarette. It might be the latest film or pop star. It might be the best friend, the latest girlfriend or boyfriend. Whoever it might be, you need to make your children realize that those people are not smoking because they choose to.

Be particularly sceptical of casual or occasional drug takers. Remember the 6 paragraphs in Chapter 3: the principle applies to all drugs, not just nicotine. Casual users try to convey the impression that they are in control and can take or leave the drug. Remember, all drug users feel stupid. They know instinctively that they didn't need the drug before they started taking it and don't understand why they now have to take it on certain occasions, even though in the early days, those occasions are few and far between. This is why all drug takers are liars. Usually they are not lying to persuade you to fall into the trap, but to try to cover up their feeling of stupidity. A classic example is: 'Oh, I can go all week without a cigarette.' Heavy smokers envy such people. Non-smokers might be tempted to take that first experimental cigarette in the belief that they won't get hooked. But just analyse the statement. If I said to you: 'Oh, I can go all week without eating a carrot,' am I telling you that I have no problem with carrots? If that is so, why do I even make the statement? Genuine non-smokers don't brag about the fact that they never need to smoke. In fact their problem is trying to understand why anyone should want to. Ironically, smokers also have that problem. No, I would only make such a statement if I had a problem with carrots, and if casual smokers can truly go all week without a cigarette, why do they need to smoke at the end of the week? After all, if you genuinely enjoy smoking a cigarette or taking a drug, why deprive yourself for a week? If you don't enjoy it, why smoke at the end of the week?

When I was addicted to golf, I would brag about how often I played and would have dearly loved to play more often. Why is it that drug addicts, whether they be nicotine addicts or otherwise, always boast how little they smoke? There seems to be some contradiction there.

Remember, all drug addicts are liars and they also lie about the level of their intake.

6. The chain effect

Whether it be nicotine or other drugs, try to get your children to see it as it really is — not the enjoyment of the occasional cigarette, but a continuous chain of nicotine entering the body, soon to be followed by an empty, insecure feeling as the nicotine leaves the body, then having to be replaced. The whole process is so gradual to begin with that it is imperceptible but as the body builds immunity to the drug, so the intake becomes greater and greater.

Let's now move on to:

THE CONCLUSION

19 *The Conclusion*

In 1983 I discovered facts about smoking that I thought would end the scourge of smoking on this planet in a few years. In 1985, I published those facts in a book:

THE EASY WAY TO STOP SMOKING

The book was more successful than I could have imagined in my wildest dreams. It is now published in over 20 languages and has not only been a bestseller every year in the UK since it was first published by Penguin, but has been an even greater success in certain other languages.

Every week I receive dozens of letters from all over the world thanking me for the insight contained in that book. Yet amazingly, society generally appears to be just as ignorant about its revelations as it was 10 years ago when Penguin first published it.

In that book I wrote: 'There is a wind of change in society. A snowball has started that I hope this book will help turn into an avalanche. You can help too by spreading this message.'

In spite of the book's success, this hasn't happened. In 1994 I wrote another book, *The Only Way to Stop*

Smoking Permanently. There I related my disappointment that society was still completely ignorant of the true facts about smoking, the facts that would actually help to end the scourge, and that our combined efforts were no more than a drop in the ocean.

I am writing this on 12 August. Grouse shooters call it the Glorious Twelfth. A few more years have passed and still our combined efforts are no more than a drop in the ocean. I love receiving letters and thanks from readers, they are a great inspiration to me. But I'm nearly 63 years old now. I have an ambition to see smoking suffer the same death that snuff-taking did some 100 years ago. If I could live to see that happen before I die, I would die a happy man. If you really want to thank me, don't send me letters telling me how grateful you are, and more power to my elbow, and asking me what you can do to help. I can't do it alone! I'll tell you what you can do to help: in the appendix I've listed the facts about smoking that society in general is still ignorant of. I not only need you to make your children aware of those facts so that they don't fall into the pit, I also need feed-back from you. I need to know how successful you were, the factors that you felt were of particular help and any criticisms you have. If you feel I can be of further assistance, please don't hesitate to write to me.

However, what I most need of you is not only to convince your own children of the truths in the appendix, but to spread the message to society generally in any way that you can, because once society realizes that drugs convey no crutch or pleasure whatsoever, that they do the complete opposite and that the human body is already fully equipped, not only to enjoy life but to cope with stress, this evil in our society will suffer the same death as snuff-taking did.

That was nicotine addiction. That was once considered to be a perfectly acceptable and sociable pastime. Just as you had the silver cigarette cases and lighters, so you had silver snuff-boxes. When did you last see a silver cigarette case? As smoking becomes more unsociable, even the expensive lighters are becoming a thing of the past. It's all short-term throwaways nowadays.

Do you really believe that snuff-takers sniffed dried tobacco up their noses to satisfy a terrible urge to sniff? If so, you presumably believe that coke addicts sniff cocaine not because they are addicted to the drug, but because they enjoy sniffing.

Do you believe that heroin addicts actually enjoy plunging a hypodermic syringe into their veins? Or do you believe they do it to try to end the withdrawal pangs from heroin?

Do you believe that smokers actually enjoy inhaling filthy, poisonous fumes into their lungs, or do you think a more logical explanation is that they are addicted to nicotine?

I sincerely hope that this book will help you to ensure that your children don't fall for the drug trap, or if they have already fallen for it, that it will help them to find it easy to escape.

1. That a healthy, human body is incomplete and requires drugs or pills to enjoy life or cope with stress and that some people have addictive personalities.

Not so. It is the drug that addicts people, not their personalities. No healthy person needs a drug before they take it, nor will they need it after they remove all the brainwashing. You won't find a smoker that likes the thought of their children smoking, which means they all wish they were non-smokers.

2. That smokers choose to smoke and to take other drugs and that they get some pleasure or benefit from them.

No, they might choose to take the first experimental dose but if they continue they do so it is because the drug has fooled them into believing that they get a genuine pleasure or crutch.

3. That nicotine or other addiction is merely habit and that casual 'users' can control and enjoy their intake.

No, the habitual behaviour results from the addiction and not vice versa. Casual 'users' are more addicted than heavy 'users' because they don't yet realize that they are addicted. They are in exactly the same position as the fly that has just begun to taste the nectar in the pitcher-plant. Except that with drugs the addict, far from imbibing nectar, isn't even imbibing food, but POISON!

4. That cutting down helps you to quit.

Just the reverse. The only reason the addict continues to take the drug is to relieve the aggravation of the craving caused by the previous dose. Just like a hunger for food, the longer you suffer it, the greater the pleasure when you finally relieve it, so the longer you suffer the craving for a poison, the greater the illusion of pleasure when you finally relieve it, and the lower the intake of a poison, the lower the desire to quit.

5. That substitutes help you to quit.

On the contrary, substitutes merely reinforce the illusion that helped you to get hooked in the first place – the belief that the human body is incomplete. If the substitute happens to contain the drug that you are trying to quit, it prolongs not only your mental addiction, but your physical addiction.

6. That smoking helps you to reduce weight.

Another fallacy. Many very heavy smokers are grossly overweight. The reason why many smokers put on weight when they attempt to quit is that for a few days their bodies continue to crave nicotine. This is identical to a hunger for food, so they substitute food for nicotine. However, one will not satisfy the other; the effect is that not only do they gain weight, they don't even relieve the empty feeling. Non-smokers don't suffer the empty feeling caused by nicotine withdrawal, and any slight inconvenience caused to smokers when they quit is caused not because they quit, but because they started.

7. That quitting drugs involves severe physical withdrawal pains.

No, even with heroin the problem is mainly mental. It's the misery caused by believing you are being deprived of a genuine pleasure or crutch. The actual physical withdrawal pains from nicotine are so slight, we only know them as: 'I need something to do with my hands', or: 'I want a cigarette.'

8. That there is pleasure in the whole ritual of smoking a cigarette – purely for ritual's sake.

Smokers tend to believe that there is an intrinsic pleasure in smoking, purely for smoking's sake, and that the health risks, money, filth and slavery are merely annoying side-effects. No, the belief that the ritual of smoking is pleasant in itself arises because that is the ritual smokers have to go through in order to get nicotine. If you believe the ritual is intrinsically pleasant, then you should have no difficulty in believing it is just as pleasant to put the burning cigarette in your ear. You should also find no difficulty in believing that snuff-takers enjoyed sniffing dried tobacco up their noses purely for the joy of sniffing, and that heroin addicts actually enjoy the ritual of sticking needles into their veins.

9. That drug addicts have to endure a transitional period of deprivation after taking the final dose and that they never feel completely free.

If, before they take what they hope will be the final dose, they believe that they are intrinsically incomplete, that the drug they are 'giving up' will genuinely help to fill the void, that it is necessary to endure a transitional period of misery and that they can never be completely free, then it would be very surprising if they didn't endure a transitional period of misery and were never in fact completely free. It would be equally surprising if, sooner or later, they weren't back on the drug again. However, if you first explain the nature of the trap, remove all the above fallacies and also explain, not only why it is not necessary to endure a transitional period of deprivation but why it is possible for any addict to feel completely and permanently free the moment they take their last dose of the drug, then they will actually be free immediately and permanently.

10. That it takes willpower to quit drugs.

Of course it does if you have a desire to take the drug, and if you retain any of the above misconceptions, you might retain a desire to continue to take the drug. But remove them all and you will remove all need or desire to take the drug. Why should you need willpower to resist a temptation that you no longer have, particularly when you have removed the final fallacy:

THAT IT IS DIFFICULT TO QUIT DRUGS?

Just read down the list of misconceptions, assuming that they are all true. Wouldn't that explain why our children get hooked, why drug addicts fear the mere thought of attempting to quit and why so many of those who do manage to escape are so easily entrapped again?

When I first set out to cure the world of smoking some 14 years ago, I believed that I was up against a very powerful enemy: the tobacco industry. Ironically, the real enemies turned out to be the very institutions that I thought would be my allies: the media, the government, ASH, QUIT and of course smokers themselves. My main enemy turned out to be the institution that I thought would be my chief ally: the established medical profession.

I was honoured to be invited to conduct a workshop at the 10th World Conference On Tobacco and Health held at Beijing in August 1997. I cannot describe how excited I felt at the prospect of hearing and of being heard by the world's leading experts on nicotine addiction.

However, that level of excitement was succeeded and exceeded by immense frustration. It was obvious that at this conference alone there had been a massive amount of thought, research and dedication devoted to alleviating the effects of nicotine addiction. Umpteen slides of various studies were produced. Even if the results were reliable, with the majority of the studies I found myself thinking: 'What was the object of the study? How does it help us to solve the problem?'

The medical profession is so wrapped up in and bound by its own procedures that it seems incapable of applying plain common sense. It reminds me of an article by 'Beachcomber' that I read many years ago: 'These ill-informed ignoramuses think that just because the price of food, rent, petrol and everything else has gone up, the cost of living has gone up, whereas the cost of living index clearly shows that in fact it has gone down.'

I prepared a questionnaire which contained 23 of the common misconceptions on the true facts about smoking. On average the medical professionals got 17 of the 23 answers wrong. Is it surprising that so many youngsters get hooked? The most disturbing aspect was their continued recommendation of nicotine replacement therapy (NRT).

During the 14 years since the Raynes Park clinic was established, the only time that the number of smokers who sought our help did not show a marked increase over the previous year coincided with the massive launch of nicotine patches. The most common comment from smokers who tried the patch was: 'It helped to keep down the terrible physical withdrawal pains, but didn't help with the psychological problem.' We could have told them that in advance. It wasn't the patch that removed the physical withdrawal pains – there are no severe physical withdrawal pangs from nicotine.

The nicotine patch bubble soon burst, as had the nicotine gum fallacy. The feedback we have been receiving from smokers in recent years is that nicotine substitutes don't work. Our cessation workshop came under the heading of: CESSATION – NON-PHARMACEUTICAL APPROACH. Originally, there were to be 7 of us conducting the workshop. I was delighted that we were grouped with other people who also advocated a non-pharmaceutical approach, as I envisaged violent conflicts of opinion over NRT.

Eventually, the group was split into 2 separate workshops. The first workshop was conducted by 4 of the doctors. Not only did every one of them advocate NRT, but one actually prescribed anti-depressants. I pointed out some of the misconceptions about NRT, in particular querying the logic of attempting to cure someone of nicotine addiction by prescribing the drug that you are attempting to cure them of. None of the queries that I made was addressed. The doctor concerned positively concluded that there was no doubt that nicotine substitutes assisted cessation, the only problem being that it was impossible to know which smokers would benefit from it. I pointed out that his statement was a contradiction. How could he state that nicotine substitutes assisted if he didn't know which smokers they would assist? This did not create the slightest chink in his assertion; I got the standard response: more research is needed.

My colleague Robin Hayley and I were grouped with just one other doctor. We supplied him with details of our method and a copy of what we intended to say prior to the conference. I was concerned that we would contradict each other and requested that he reciprocate. He didn't. Even after hearing his discourse, I haven't the vaguest notion of his method. Before the workshop I asked him his opinion of NRT and was relieved to be told that he believed that it didn't work. My relief was short-lived when he followed up with: 'However, I do sometimes recommend it.' Robin asked him why he recommended something that he believed didn't work. His reply was that smokers needed something. I regret that this was typical of the presentations that Robin and I attended.

It seems to me that this is the characteristic attitude of the medical profession to quitting smoking, because they don't understand the true nature of nicotine addiction. Their advice is: 'Try this, if it doesn't work, try that, try anything and everything.' I hope this isn't the typical attitude to other medical problems. We are entitled to expect better from anyone who purports to be an expert on a particular subject. We expect an expert to advise us on true facts and not misconceptions, and to inform us of the most effective method to quit. The truth is that, apart from the doctors who recommend my method, doctors have no notion of what is the most effective method and they should be honest enough to admit to that fact.

Because the majority of smokers have seen through the NRT fallacy, I assumed that the physicians had followed suit. One of the questions we asked was: do you believe nicotine replacement helps smokers to quit? The answer was a unanimous yes.

I pointed out the following facts:

1. That snuff-taking was the previous century's version of nicotine addiction and that it died because of NRT – it was replaced by the manufactured cigarette.

2. That telling smokers not to smoke nicotine because smoking is dangerous, but to chew it instead, is equivalent to advising heroin addicts not to smoke heroin but to inject it into a vein.

3. That NRT is based on the principle that when a smoker attempts to quit, he has two powerful enemies to conquer. The first is to break the habit. The second is to survive the terrible physical withdrawal pangs. If you have two powerful enemies to defeat, it makes sense to fight them one at a time. So you quit smoking and while you are breaking the habit you keep the body supplied with nicotine. Once you've broken the habit you wean yourself off the nicotine. The theory sounds marvellous but:

   a. Exactly the same effect can be achieved by gradually cutting down on smoking and any smoker knows that cutting down makes it harder.

   b. It's based on incorrect facts. The habit of smoking doesn't exist. Smoking is merely nicotine addiction. All you are trying to achieve when you quit smoking is to starve the little physical nicotine monster inside your body and remove the big nicotine monster inside your head in the shortest possible time. NRT keeps the little monster alive which in turn keeps the big monster alive. The second point is that the

physical withdrawal pains from nicotine are so mild
that they are almost imperceptible and that NRT is
unnecessary.

4. That all substitutes are bad because they perpetuate
the illusion that the smoker is making a sacrifice.
NRT has the additional advantage of keeping the
ex-smoker addicted to nicotine.

5. That many nicotine addicts attend our clinics because
they are addicted to nicotine gum.

All these facts were like water off a duck's back. These
scientific doctors offer no counter-arguments but just
stick rigidly to the results of scientific evaluations. You
point out that their evaluations are based on unscientific
facts:

1. For the evaluation to be effective the smokers should
not be aware whether they are receiving NRT or
the placebo, but it would become blatantly obvious
the moment they received the initial dose.

2. In any event the period of abstinence is calculated
from the date of the last cigarette. It should be based
on the date that the ex-smoker stops taking nicotine.
One would expect smokers who continue to take nicotine in another form, whether it be through cigars,
pipe or NRT, to abstain longer from cigarettes.

3. The use of NRT is merely an extension of the willpower method which is in itself incredibly ineffective.
It might well be that NRT makes the willpower
method less ineffective. That is no excuse for advocat-

ing it. A runner will find it difficult if his legs are tied together (willpower method). A pair of crutches will help (NRT). However, untie the legs (Allen Carr's method) and the crutches become a handicap.

Even if you ignored all the obvious flaws in the NRT evaluations and accepted the claims, the results are somewhat pathetic compared to a method that will enable any smoker to quit easily, instantaneously and permanently.

It seemed to us that the bulk of the conference was an advert for NRT. They even use the same techniques to sell nicotine addiction that the tobacco industry has been banned from using – glamorous women wearing a patch or about to chew nicotine gum, and can it be just coincidence that the patches are marketed in a packet the exact size and shape of a packet of cigarettes? If the NRT industry is genuinely trying to help smokers quit, why do they need to resort to such tactics?

The glossy Nicorette brochure contains a copy of Dr Fagerstrom's Tolerance questionnaire. It is similar to one of the typical questionnaires that appear regularly in the tabloid press designed to help you decide whether the opposite sex finds you attractive. This one is designed to help you decide how dependent a smoker is on nicotine. In his lecture, Dr Fagerstrom commenced by explaining that he didn't know how to decide whether a smoker was dependent on nicotine or not. However, his questionnaire assumes that all smokers are. A score of 7 or over indicates high nicotine dependence, 6 or under indicates low, and the maximum is 11. Considering I've yet to meet a smoker that is as dependent as I was and that Robin was on 60 a day, you would expect my score to be 11 and Robin's to be around 9. But my score was 3 and Robin's 5.

However, the NRT advocates treat this table as gospel and no amount of plain common sense can shake their faith in it. Another highly respected and eminent doctor actually stated on national TV that it is possible that some ex-smokers will be dependent on NRT for the rest of their lives. How can qualified doctors preach such nonsense? You don't need to be a doctor to know that human beings are not dependent upon poisons. This is the main flaw in the scientific evaluations of the medical profession – they get so involved with the intricacies of the process that even when the conclusion results in what is obviously nonsense, they actually believe in the nonsense; even worse, their colleagues meekly accept their conclusions as gospel.

How does the medical profession explain how Carr and Hayley and all the other heavy smokers we have helped to quit stopped overnight without any withdrawal symptoms or use of NRT? Even more important: why don't they even bother to ask us?

Now read again the misconceptions listed at the beginning of this appendix, seeing each item as it really is: an illusion. Do you really believe that your children would be stupid enough to fall for the trap if they knew all the facts? And if they were already hooked, do you think they'd find it difficult to escape?

I assure you that once all the illusions have been removed, it's not only easy but you can enjoy the whole process right from taking the final dose and feel permanently free immediately. Being dependent on a drug is equivalent to being imprisoned for life. You feel that you are both the prisoner and the gaoler and you feel stupid because you feel instinctively that you have the power to release yourself from the prison and can't understand why you can't do it.

In fact you are not your own gaoler. What actually imprisons you is not the physical effect of the drug itself, but the subtlety of the trap, the brainwashing, the misconceptions. It is essential that you and your children are satisfied that all the misconceptions that I have listed above are just that – misconceptions.

For years I've been a lone voice trying to educate society about these misconceptions. The medical profession is quite rightly highly respected by the rest of society, we are entitled to rely on their knowledge and expertise. In spite of the fact that this large, respected, trusted and powerful institution has preached and continues to preach the exact opposite to the true facts, I have managed to achieve a high level of success. Just think how quickly the whole insidious scourge of drug addiction would be removed from our society if the medical profession proclaimed the true facts.

Our children and grandchildren will not be truly safe until that object has been achieved. I need your help in this matter. Every time you hear an individual, listen to a radio or TV programme or read an article which perpetuates the illusions about drug addiction, please make the effort to contradict them. Encourage your friends and relatives to do the same. Remember, the Great Barrier Reef is made up of tiny polyps which cannot be seen with the naked eye, but the total reef can be seen from the moon. United we cannot fail.

The explanations that I have given to account for the fallacy of the misconceptions are brief and in some cases might require further elaboration. If so, please refer to the appropriate chapters in *The Only Way to Stop Smoking Permanently*. If you still have any doubts, telephone our Raynes Park clinic.

I'm often asked how my life was changed when I quit smoking: did I miss cigarettes or have occasional cravings? Did I miss them? It was like being released from a misty, black and white world of fear and depression into a colourful world of sunshine, health and freedom. Can you imagine how the Count of Monte Cristo felt, locked up in that prison for 14 years believing he could never be free, then suddenly realizing he was free? I've had some marvellous experiences in my life, but by far the greatest:

IS THE JOY OF ESCAPING FROM THE SLAVERY OF DRUG ADDICTION!

I sincerely hope that our joint efforts will enable your children, and all others, to avoid the misery and slavery of drug addiction and help any who have already fallen into the trap, whether they be 9 or 90, to escape.

ALLEN CARR UK

LONDON
1c Amity Grove
Raynes Park
London SW20 0LQ
Tel. & Fax: 0181 944 7761
Therapist: John Dicey

BIRMINGHAM
415 Hagley Road West
Quinton
Birmingham B32 2AD
Tel. & Fax: 0121 423 1227
Therapist: Jason Vale
E-mail:
JASEYBEAN@AOL.COM

SOUTH COAST
Christchurch Business Centre
Grange Road
Dorset BH23 4JD
Tel.: 01425 272757
Fax: 01425 274250
Therapist: Anne Emery
Email: AEmery3192@aol.com

YORKSHIRE
Leeds
Tel.: 0113 235 0000
Fax: 01904 340 159
Therapist: Diana Evans

YORK
185 Burton Stone Lane
York YO3 6DG

Tel.: 0700 900 0305
Fax: 01904 340 159
Therapist: Diana Evans

SHEFFIELD
Tel.: 0700 900 0305
Fax: 01904 304 159
Therapist: Diana Evans

NORTH EAST
10 Dale Terrace
Dalton-le-Dale
Seaham
County Durham SR7 8QP
Tel. & Fax: 0191 581 0449
Therapist: Tony Attrill

BRISTOL
Unit 13, The Coach House
2 Upper York Street
Bristol BS2 8QN
Tel.: 0117 908 1106
Therapist: John Emery

WALES
Travellers Chambers
Ludlow Street
Penarth
S. Glamorgan CF64 1ED
Tel.: 01222 705500
Fax: 0181 940 1153
Therapist: Jim Trimmer
E-mail:
jimtrim@compuserve.com

DEVON
Angel Cottage
Cutteridge Farm
Whitestone
Exeter EX4 2HE
Tel.: 01392 811603
Therapist: Trevor Emdon
E-mail:
horwell@curobell.co.uk

EDINBURGH
48 Eastfield
Joppa
Edinburgh EH15 2PN
Tel. & Fax: 0131 660 6688
Therapist: Derek McGuff
E-mail:
derek@djmcg.demon.co.uk

KENT
Tel.: 01622 679 595
Therapist: Angela Jouanneau

ALLEN CARR
HOLLAND

AMSTERDAM
Pythagorasstraat 22
1098 GC Amsterdam
Tel.: 020 465 4665
Fax: 020 465 6682
Therapist: Eveline De Mooij

UTRECHT
De Beaufortlaan 22 B
3768 MJ Soestduinen
(gem. Soest)
Tel. (stop smoking): 035 60
29458

Tel. (weight): 035 60 32153
Fax: 035 60 32265
Therapist: Nicolette de Boer
E-mail:
nicolette@overtoom.com

ROTTERDAM
Mathenesserlaan 290
3021 HV Rotterdam
Tel.: 010 244 07 09
Fax: 010 244 07 10
Therapist: Kitty van't Hof

ALLEN CARR ITALY

MILAN
c/o Studio Pavanello
Piazza Argentina 4
20124 Milan
Tel.: 02 29 52 9251
Therapist: Francesca Cesati

ALLEN CARR FRANCE

MARSEILLE
70 Rue St Ferreol
13006 Marseille
Tel.: 04 91 33 54 55
Fax: 04 91 33 32 77
Therapist: Erick Serre
E-mail: ELYFRANCE@
COMPUSERVE.COM

ALLEN CARR
AUSTRALIA

MELBOURNE
148 Central Road
Nunawading
Victoria 3131

Tel. & Fax: 03 9894 8866
Therapist: Trudy Ward
E-mail:
easywaya@Bigpond.com

ALLEN CARR USA

TEXAS
12823 Kingsbridge Lane
Houston
Texas 77077
Tel.: 281 597 1904
Fax: 281 597 9829
Therapist: Laura Cattell
E-mail: ACatt38826@aol.com

ST LOUIS
Tel. & Fax: 314 567 4505
Therapist: Keith Newmark
E-mail: acezway@swbell.net

ALLEN CARR ISRAEL

JERUSALEM
97 Jaffa Street
Office 806
Jerusalem
Tel.: 02 624 2586
Therapist: Michael Goldman

ALLEN CARR HONG KONG

CAUSEWAY BAY
22nd Floor A & B
Guangdong Tours Centre
18 Pennington Street
Causeway Bay

Tel.: 852 2893 1571
Fax: 852 2554 2958
Therapists: Leo Ngai & Jon
Lewis-Evans
E-mail: easyway@ukwww.com

ALLEN CARR CANADA

TORONTO
461 North Service Road
Unit B7
Oakville
Ontario L6M 2V5
Tel.: 905 827 3888
Fax: 905 827 9434
Therapist: Nancy Toth
E-mail: aceasyway@msn.com

ALLEN CARR GERMANY

Website: http://
www.allen-carr.de
E-mail: info@allen-carr.de

MUNICH
Hochgstattweg 8
82216 Uberacker
Tel.: 081 35 8466
Fax: 081 35 8920
Therapists: Petra Wackerle &
Stephan Kraus

STUTTGART
Heumadener Str. 11
70329 Stuttgart-Hedelfingen
Tel.: 0711 4209154
Fax: 08135 8920
Therapists: Petra Wackerle &
Stephan Kraus

HAMBURG
Tel.: 040 280 510 56
Therapist: Regina Hildebrandt
E-mail: info@allen-carr.de

BAD SALZUFLEN
Im neuen Land 20a
32107 Bad Salzuflen
Tel.: 05222 797 622
Fax: 05222 797 624
Therapist: Wolfgang Rinke
E-mail:
wolfgang.rinke@allen-carr.de

DUSSELDORF
Steffenstr. 4, 40545
Düsseldorf
Tel.: 0211 557 1738
Fax: 0211 557 1740
Therapist: Axel Matheja
E-mail:
axel.matheja@allen-carr.de

BERLIN
Tel.: 030 217 50488
Fax: 030 217 50489
E-mail: info@allen-carr.de

FRANKFURT
Tel.: 06701 960673
Therapist: Elfi Blume
E-mail:
elfi.blume@allen-carr.de

ALLEN CARR AUSTRIA

Website: http://
www.allen-carr.at

VIENNA
Tel.: 01 3331355
Fax: 08031 463068
Therapist: Erich Kellermann
E-mail:
erich.kellermann@allen-carr.at

SALZBURG
Tel.: 662 878718
Fax: 08031 463068
Therapist: Erich Kellermann
E-mail:
erich.kellermann@allen-carr.at

ALLEN CARR SWITZERLAND

Website: http://
www.allen-carr.ch

ZURICH
Bernhofstr. 34, Ch-8134
Adliswil
Tel.: 0041 1 7105678
Fax: 0041 1 7105683
Therapist: Cyrill Argast
E-mail:
cyrill.argast@allen-carr.ch

ALLEN CARR BELGIUM

ANTWERP
Marialei 47
2018 Antwerpen
Tel.: 03 281 6255
Fax: 03 744 0608
Therapist: Dirk Nielandt
E-mail: GD32280@GLO.BE

ALLEN CARR SPAIN

MADRID
C/Fernandez De Los Rios
106, 1. IZQ
28015 Madrid
Tel.: 91 543 8504
Therapist: Geoffrey Molloy &
Rhea Sivi
E-mail: sivimoll@arrakis.es

ALLEN CARR ICELAND

REYKJAVIK
Losheimar 4
104 Reykjavik
Tel.: 354 553 9590
Fax: 354 588 7060
Therapists: Petur Einarsson &
Valgeir Skagfjord
E-mail: pein@ismennt.is

ALLEN CARR IRELAND

DUBLIN
123 Coolamber Park
Templeogue
Dublin 16
Tel.: 01 494 1644
Therapist: Brenda Sweeney
E-mail: seanow@iol

ALLEN CARR SOUTH AFRICA

CAPETOWN
P.O. Box 5269
Helderberg
Somerset West 7135
Tel.: 083 600 5555
Fax: 083 8 600 5555
Therapist: Dr Charles Nel

ALLEN CARR ECUADOR

QUITO
Veintimilla 878 y
Amazonas
PO Box 17-03-179
Quito
Tel. & Fax: 02 56 33 44
Tel.: 02 82 09 20
Therapist: Ingrid Wittich